£.95

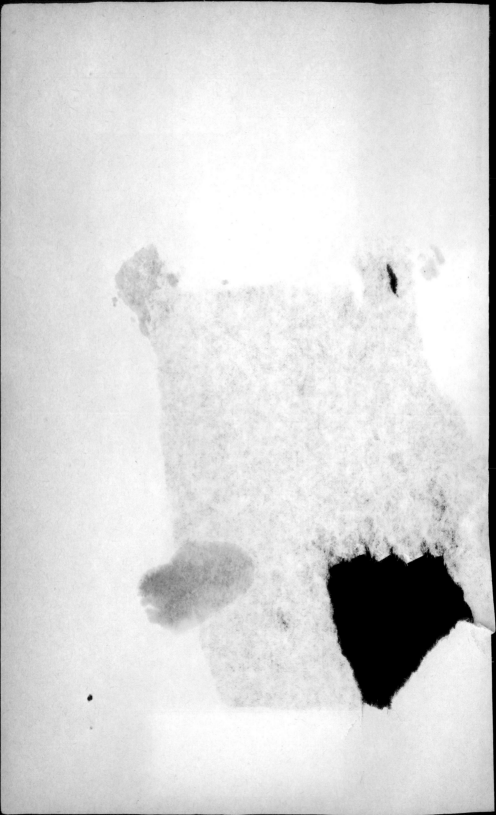

Ted Hughes

Open Guides to Literature

Series Editor: Graham Martin (Professor of Literature, The Open University)

Titles in the Series

Angus Calder: Byron
Jenni Calder: *Animal Farm* and *1984*
Walford Davies: Dylan Thomas
Roger Day: Larkin
Peter Faulkner: Yeats: *The Tower* and *The Winding Stair*
P. N. Furbank: Pound
Graham Holderness: *Hamlet*
Graham Holderness: *Women in Love*
Graham Holderness: *Wuthering Heights*
Jeannette King: *Jane Eyre*
Graham Martin: *Great Expectations*
Dennis Walder: Hughes
Roderick Watson: MacDiarmid

Ted Hughes giving a reading at the Round House, London.

DENNIS WALDER

Ted Hughes

Open University Press

Milton Keynes · Philadelphia

Open University Press
Open University Eductional Enterprises Limited
12 Cofferidge Close
Stony Stratford
Milton Keynes MK11 1BY, England

and

242 Cherry Street
Philadelphia, PA 19106, USA

First Published 1987

British Library Cataloguing in Publication Data
Walder, Dennis
   Ted Hughes. — (Open guides to literature).
   1.   Hughes, Ted — Criticism and
interpretation
   I.   Title
   821'.914   PR6058.U37Z/

   ISBN 0–335–15113–2

   ISBN 0–335–15112–4 Pbk

Library of Congress Cataloging in Publication Data
Walder, Dennis.
   Ted Hughes.
   (Open guides to literature)
   Bibliography: p.
   Includes index.
   1.   Hughes, Ted, 1930– —Criticism and
interpretation.   I. Title. II. Series.
PR6058.U37Z93   1987   821'.914   87–22071

ISBN 0–335–15113–2

ISBN 0–335–15112–4 (pbk.)

Project management: Clarke Williams
Printed in Great Britain

Contents

Series Editor's Preface

The intention of this series is to provide short introductory books about major writers, texts, and literary concepts for students of courses in Higher Education which substantially or wholly involve the study of Literature.

The series adopts a pedagogic approach and style similar to that of Open University Material for Literature courses. *Open Guides* aim to inculcate the reading 'skills' which many introductory books in the field tend, mistakenly, to assume that the reader already possesses. They are, in this sense, 'teacherly' texts, planned and written in a manner which will develop in the reader the confidence to undertake further independent study of the topic. They are 'open' in two senses. First, they offer a three-way tutorial exchange between the writer of the *Guide*, the text or texts in question, and the reader. They invite readers to join in an exploratory discussion of texts, concentrating on their key aspects and on the main problems which readers, coming to the texts for the first time, are likely to encounter. The flow of a *Guide* 'discourse' is established by putting questions for the reader to follow up in a tentative and searching spirit, guided by the writer's comments, but not dominated by an over-arching and single-mindedly-pursued argument or evaluation, which itself requires to be 'read'.

Guides are also 'open' in a second sense. They assume that literary texts are 'plural', that there is no end to interpretation, and that it is for the reader to undertake the pleasurable task of discovering meaning and value in such texts. *Guides* seek to provide, in compact form, such relevant biographical, historical and cultural information as bears upon the reading of the text, and they point the reader to a selection of the best available critical discussions of it. They are not in themselves concerned to propose, or to counter, particular readings of the texts, but rather to put *Guide* readers in a position to do that for themselves. Experienced travellers learn to dispense with guides, and so it should be for readers of this series.

This *Open Guide* will be most usefully studied in conjunction with
Ted Hughes's *Selected Poems: 1957–1981* (Faber, 1982.)

Acknowledgements

My thanks go to the Open University for permission to develop this book from material originally contributed to their Twentieth Century Poetry Course: specifically, Chapters 1 and 5 have been developed from my 'course unit' on *Ted Hughes and Sylvia Plath* (1976) and Chapter 6 from my radio broadcast 'Crow' (1977). The series editor, Graham Martin, who was also chairman of that course, has made helpful suggestions all along. I would also like to thank Donna Forster and Maureen Mulligan.

Grateful acknowledgement is also made to the following for permission to quote copyright material: to Faber and Faber Ltd., for poems and extracts from *The Hawk in the Rain, Lupercal, Wodwo, Crow, Season Songs, Gaudete, Moon Bells* (published by Chatto and Windus), *Cave Birds, Remainins of Elmet, Moortown, Selected Poems, River, What Is The Truth?* and *Flowers and Insects* by Ted Hughes; and for extracts from *Wallace Stevens: Selected Poems, T. S. Eliot: Collected Poems 1909–1962,* and *Seamus Heaney: Preoccupations: Selected Prose 1968–1978;* to Harper & Row, Publishers, Inc., for selected poems and lines of poetry from *New Selected Poems* by Ted Hughes © 1982 by Ted Hughes, *The Hawk in the Rain* by Ted Hughes © 1956, 1957 by Ted Hughes, *Lupercal* by Ted Hughes © 1958, 1959, 1960 by Ted Hughes, *Crow: From the Life and Songs of the Crow* by Ted Hughes © 1971 Ted Hughes, *Gaudete* by Ted Hughes © 1977 by Ted Hughes, *Remains of Elmet* by Ted Hughes and Fay Godwin © 1979 by Ted Hughes, *What Is The Truth?* by Ted Hughes © 1984 by Ted Hughes and *River: New Poems* by Ted Hughes © 1983 by Ted Hughes; to Viking/Penguin Inc., for extracts from *Moon Whales: And other Moon Poems, Season Songs* and *Cave-Birds* by Ted Hughes, and 'The Mosquito' by D. H. Lawrence; to Alfred A. Knopf. Inc. for an extract from *Flowers and Insects* by Ted Hughes, and for an extract from 'Thirteen Ways of Looking at a Blackbird' from *The Collected Poems of Wallace Stevens* ©; to Harcourt, Brace Jovanovich, Inc. for an extract from *T. S. Eliot: Collected Poems 1909–1962;* to Mrs. Clare Blunden for 'Midnight Skaters' by Edmund Blunden; to Anvil Press Poetry for 'The Dream of the Quartz Pebble' by Vasko Popa, translated by Anne Pennington; and to Cambridge University Press for extracts from Keith Sagar, *The Art of Ted Hughes*, second edn.

Grateful acknowledgements is also made to the following for illustrations: to R. J. Lloyd for permission to use as part of the cover design an illustration from *What Is The Truth?* by Ted Hughes; to Mary Elgin/Report, for 'Ted Hughes giving a reading at the Round House' (frontispiece); to the Trustees of the Imperial War Museum, London, for permission to reproduce the First World War photograph on p. 32; to the Museum of Modern Art, New York, for Joan Miró: *Person Throwing a Stone at a Bird*, © ADAGP 1987 reproduced on p. 57; and to Olwyn Hughes, for permission to reproduce the Leonard Baskin drawing of a crow reproduced on p. 62.

1.   Introduction

On 19 December 1984, Ted Hughes became Poet Laureate, in succession to the late John Betjeman. He thereby joined the long line of English poets stretching back to Ben Jonson who have been thus honoured. Within half an hour of the news, 2,000 copies of his *Selected Poems* were sold, and within two days his publishers had ensured that a further 15,000 copies were printed and available for sale. Profiles and interviews followed in quick succession and, before the week was out, a new poem in a Sunday newspaper (*The Observer*) with a readership of over half a million. The poem was a 'Rain-Charm for the Duchy: A Blessed, Devout Drench for the Christening of Prince Harry',

In this way the poet of extremes, of those amoral, primitive drives which (it is the main thrust of his work to suggest) underlie our culture, becomes, apparently, assimilated by that culture. This book participates in the same process: by trying to define, interpret and evaluate Hughes, it confirms his status. If, as I intend to, I point out the subversive force of certain images in his work, I simultaneously rob them of some of that force. If, as I intend to, I suggest the problems raised by a reading of his poetry, I simultaneously help to smooth them out. There is no escape from this paradox. On the other hand, you the reader, are free to see what is happening and to counter it. This you can do by going to Hughes's poems and trying out, modifying or rejecting my proposed readings. You can also go to other critics and commentators, find out what they say, argue with them, and come back and argue with what I say here. It is then, very important that, if this is to be more than merely another stone on the cairn erected upon Ted Hughes by our culture, you should read carefully, and with trust in your own responses and ideas, the poems discussed and referred to here. You should also read more widely and, if possible, some at least of the criticism that is available. None of us reads without preconceived ideas and assumptions, and good criticism can help us become aware of what those are, and help us develop a more independent position. I should say that I have here tried to suggest some of the problems which, it seems to me, understanding the multiple and shifting meanings of poetic texts will raise — especially the issue of the author's intentions. This is by way of recognising that, as more recent criticism has tried to bring out, any text that survives is constantly being read and re-read — or *consumed* — in a plurality of (often competing) ways, depending upon who is doing the reading, when, and under what material and ideological circumstances.

I will use Ted Hughes's *Selected Poems: 1957–1981* for most of my detailed discussion; but I will also refer to other poems and collections of poems by Hughes, as well as to some of his non-poetic output. There is probably no better way of getting to know a poet's work than by trying to grapple with all of it – including, if any, what is written in other genres or produced in other media. The achievement of poets is primarily an achievement of *language*: of a way of writing which, at its most intense, finds its way into poetry, but which also runs into prose, drama, fiction, letters or, perhaps, all utterances both private and public. So all of this could be grist to the mill. But, although I will be using some of Hughes's criticism, his translations (his versions of translations, to be precise), his children's books, plays, stories, and some of his own recorded remarks about himself and his work, my main focus will remain his poetry. This is what matters most.

Readers today can respond with the pleasure of immediate recognition ('Yes, this is what I feel') to the poetry of fifty or sixty years ago, to the poetry of Hardy, Yeats or Eliot; even, perhaps, to the poetry of their predecessors, such as Tennyson or Browning. But there is a unique potential in the poetry of our own time to reach us and move us: not only by exploring our everyday social and political preoccupations, although this is valuable, but also by touching the deeper springs of fear and hope which lie beneath, and which we dimly sense within ourselves as we live on into the last decades of the twentieth century. It was the critic F.R. Leavis's insistent belief (best expressed in his *New Bearings in English Poetry*, first published in 1932) that contemporary verse should be studied as the finest, most concentrated, and powerful articulation of current modes of feeling and experience. This overstates the case for poetry: other literary forms have a claim too, not to mention the other arts. But, without being a 'Leavisite', it is possible to argue that Hughes (for one) is particularly remarkable for the fierce power, concentration, and control with which he has tapped the potential of poetry now.

If I were to be asked to single out one element in his work which most exemplifies this, I would say it is *surprise*: the almost physical shock of awareness, of recognition, which his best poems generate in the reader/listener. What is it we are asked to recognise, or become aware of? Basically, the massive ebb and flow of natural forces which underlie life, which underlie our everyday existences. Hughes is interested in big, 'primitive' themes: Nature, War, Sex and Death. He explores them by means of image, myth and symbol.

Because many of his poems describe animals or have animals in their titles, it has long been commonly assumed that he is a kind of Zoo Laureate. But it is impossible to understand his work without recognising that the animals are not there for their own sake, however brilliantly defined they seem to be; but they serve as metaphors for a particular human vision. This vision is many-sided, but can be reduced to two fundamental, and opposing, qualities: a celebration of energy, spontaneity and instinctual drive on the one hand; and a fearful admission of the deadly, abiding predatoriness of life on the other. Sometimes these elements get confused and brutality seems to be enjoyed; more usually, there is an exercise of controlled power which enables us to respond unreservedly to Hughes's account of episodes from 'the war between vitality and death', as he puts it.[1]

There is no better way of showing what I mean than by getting down to specific, single poems, which is what I will do in the following chapters. Each chapter involves a discussion of a different aspect of Hughes's poetry, based upon a small group of individual poems analysed in some detail. It is important to remember one inevitable result of this approach: it leaves out a lot. Hughes is prolific and, at the time of writing, has no less than ten published collections of poetry to his name, excluding verse for children (although even his so-called 'farmyard fables for the young' are by no means that limited in their interest or appeal); and new poems continue to appear almost weekly. No definitive judgements can be passed on a body of work so far from complete. That is, in so far as it is possible to be definitive about literary judgements at all.

A final point: although it is the main aim of this book (as it is of others in the series to which it belongs) to highlight the issues which a careful account of the writer's work seems to rise, Hughes (like all contemporaries, perhaps) is so close to us in time and what he writes about, that there is a special danger of slotting him into some literary-critical category before really trying to attend to what his work says and how it affects us. An active critic himself, Hughes has nevertheless displayed strong suspicion of the rational, critical intellect which, he evidently believes (along with his Romantic predecessors) murders to dissect. By offering as much of his own words in what follows as I have been able to, I hope I have been more of a midwife than a murderer.

2.   'A most surprising first book'

I shall begin immediately with two examples of 'surprise', from quite different periods of Ted Hughes's career. The first is 'The Thought-Fox', often taken as one of his most characteristic and revealing poems. It first appeared in Hughes's first published collection, *The Hawk in the Rain* (1957), and he has since chosen it to stand as the lead-in to his *Selected Poems* (p. 13). Read it through carefully now, two or three times. If you can read it aloud, or listen to it read aloud, so much the better. This applies to all the poems I will discuss. Hughes himself remarked before reading some of his work on the record *The Poet Speaks* no. 5 (available on tape, too), 'I prefer poems to make an effect on being heard'. There are several recorded versions of him reading 'The Thought-Fox'. If it is familiar, as it may well be now that Hughes is so well known and widely anthologised, try nevertheless to read or listen to it with a 'fresh' eye and ear:

The Thought-Fox

I imagine this midnight moment's forest:
Something else is alive
Beside the clock's loneliness
And this blank page where my fingers move.

Through the window I see no star:
Something more near
Though deeper within darkness
Is entering the loneliness:

Cold, delicately as the dark snow,
A fox's nose touches twig, leaf;
Two eyes serve a movement, that now
And again now, and now, and now

Sets neat prints into the snow
Between trees, and warily a lame
Shadow lags by stump and in hollow
Of a body that is bold to come

Across clearings, an eye,
A widening deepening greenness,
Brilliantly, concentratedly,
Coming about its own business

Till, with a sudden sharp hot stink of fox
It enters the dark hole of the head.
The window is starless still; the clock ticks,
The page is printed.

What is your first, your immediate impression? Or, to put it another way: what, simply does this poem seem to be about? How does the last line affect your understanding of it?

DISCUSSION

My own initial response was of surprise — and excitement. I was astonished by the sharp, almost unpleasant feeling this poem evoked in me of the physical presence of a fox, brought alive as I read it by the vivid and precise details of its appearance and manner; its nose 'delicately' touching 'twig, leaf', as it emerges from the dark, its paws setting 'neat prints into the snow', with a movement enhanced by the rhythmical, hypnotic repetition of 'now/And again now, and now, and now' in the third stanza. The poem seems simply to be about a fox.

Yet, as Hughes himself points out in talking about this, 'the first "animal" poem I ever wrote', it is 'about a fox, obviously enough, but a fox that is both a fox and not a fox'.[1] The title alone suggests as much; moreover, the poem begins 'I imagine', which implies a speaker, a consciousness which the fox can inhabit as metaphor.

For Hughes, metaphor is the primary source of linguistic creativity, of the shaping, poetic imagination, and his fox is not there for its own sake, but as a means of communicating this truth. This is implicit in the most striking aspect of the poem's first impact upon being read or heard: that dramatic double-take produced by the last line, when the realization comes that the page is indeed printed, and lies before us. By means of a neat pun, the 'neat prints' of the fox's paws have become the letters and words describing them. (Listening to the poem first makes this more, rather than less, apparent.) We have been made to share the pleasurable shock of the emergence of a poem: a sharing evidently of importance to figures such as the narrator, who finds himself isolated in the dark 'loneliness' (the word is repeated) of midnight, awaiting inspiration.

This is, then, a poem about the writing or creation of a poem. I will be saying more about Hughes's place in the traditions of English poetry later. But you may well be familiar enough with the great Romantics to recognise a traditional subject here: Coleridge's 'Dejection: An Ode' (1802), provides an early example, and helps to establish the literary origin of Hughes's preoccupation in 'The Thought-Fox'. As it happens, the personal, authorial presence which the dramatic and personal quality of the poem suggests, has been testified to by Hughes, who has revealed that 'The Thought-Fox' was the product of a sudden recall of childhood memory, which came to him one night in his dreary London lodgings after a year or so without inspiration.[2] As with the first Romantics, the remembered image of childhood or youth has brought a restorative, creative impulse 'in lonely rooms, and mid the din/Of towns and cities', as Wordsworth put it ('Tintern Abbey'). But, unlike Wordsworth or Coleridge, Hughes has explored his subject with the brevity, density and stress-based rhythmical simplicity of a *modern* poet. 'The Thought-Fox' (you will notice if you go back and look at its technical elements) is tightly contained within six short four-line stanzas, quietly half-rhyming, and based on a four-stress line of eight or ten syllables; with the exception of the last line, which punches its point home with only two, strong alliterative stresses ('The páge is prínted').

The modern quality of Hughes's work is even more evident from the next poem (reprinted on p. 116 of the *Selected Poems*), written much later in his career, and apparently representative of a quite different impulse. What do you make of it? Does it also surprise you? How, generally, is it different from 'The Thought-Fox'? What familiar 'myth' does it seem to recall?

A Childish Prank

Man's and woman's bodies lay without souls,
Dully gaping, foolishly staring, inert
On the flowers of Eden.
God pondered.

The problem was so great, it dragged him asleep.

Crow laughed.
He bit the Worm, God's only son,
Into two writhing halves.

He stuffed into man the tail half
With the wounded end hanging out.

He stuffed the head half headfirst into woman
And it crept in deeper and up
To peer out through her eyes
Calling its tail-half to join up quickly, quickly
Because O it was painful.

Man awoke being dragged across the grass.
Woman awoke to see him coming.
Neither knew what had happened.

God went on sleeping.

Crow went on laughing.

DISCUSSION

Surprised? Shocked? Puzzled? Amused? I think I was all of these when I first came across this poem, in the collection *Crow* (1970, 1972). It is not easy to know what to make of it; but it is stunningly powerful, — and comic, in a dark, mockingly subversive way. What does it mock? The answer lies in its allusion to the familiar Christian account of Creation and the Fall — specifically, to Genesis, chapters 2–3. Human sexuality has been, it seems, bequeathed to mankind, not by God, but by some malicious, satanic creature for its own amusement, while God is 'sleeping'. This creature, presumably the mischievous prankster of the poem's title, has become the creator himself, and made 'the Worm, God's only son' (Christ become the serpent of sexuality) his passive victim. God's absent-minded incompetence has permitted this substitution of animal lust in place of the soul as the origin of life.

Unlike 'The Thought-Fox', this poem relies on our knowledge of a myth (in the sense of a set of beliefs embodied in a narrative) for its meaning and effect — a myth with which our culture is thoroughly infused. It is also unlike the earlier poem in its shape or structure: lines and stanzas (if one can call them that) of quite different length, unrhyming, free. 'The Thought-Fox', for all its modern qualities, seems traditional by comparison. Yet, at the same time, the feelings aroused by 'A Childish Prank' are also disturbingly familiar too: the sexual relationship imagined as a black joke played on us by some grinning malefactor, rather than the holy meeting of souls we would like it to be.

   Hughes's grisly, even surreal humour, here as elsewhere in the *Crow* series, connects less with the English poetic tradition, than with some of the recent Eastern European poets in whom he has taken an interest — János Pilinszky (whose poetry he has helped render into English), for example, or Vasko Popa. Popa writes cycles of poems upon a given theme, each a little fable of 'visionary anecdote', as Hughes calls them.[3] Like Popa, Hughes is strongly interested in the down-to-earth myths and legends of popular folklore, images of survival for our post-Holocaust, post-nuclear world. He has mounted several poem-cycle projects of this general type, asserting the need for myth to compensate humanity for its loss of instinctual direction. Whether or not he manages this successfully, he is always at his most powerful when suggesting the astonishing, energetic 'otherness' of the natural world: the 'sharp hot stink' of the fox entering the head is paralleled by the raucous, manic laughter of that crow. These are undeniably surprising, memorable images.

Edwin Muir, one of Hughes's most enthusiastic early admirers, called *The Hawk in the Rain* 'a most surprising first book'. What surprised Muir above all was Hughes's power, which he located in these terms: 'The images are so vivid that a symbolic meaning springs from them, whether it was intended to be there or not.'[4] Hughes's animal creations are always like this: their appearance suggests a state of heightened, dream-like, even hallucinatory awareness, so that the ordinary, the everyday, becomes suffused with what seems a symbolic effect, operating independently of the writer's will. Muir was referring specifically to 'The Jaguar'. It is worth looking at the poem in more detail. Read it yourself now (it is on p. 15 of *Selected Poems*), and ask yourself if Muir's view finds any echo in your own response to it. Re-reading it, you might also look for any particular word, or group of words, which may be said to generate a feeling of heightened or special awareness.

DISCUSSION

Hughes's predatory subject hurries 'enraged/Through prison darkness' before a crowd (ourselves as spectators) 'mesmerized' like a child 'at a dream'. Its power is explosive ('a short fierce fuse ... the bang of blood') but contained at least temporarily, by the cage it inhabits. Yet 'there's no cage to him/More than to the visionary his cell' and finally 'Over the cage floor the horizons come'. The jaguar's world is *the* world, as long as the poem lasts. What has begun as an evocation, brilliantly vivid but no more than that, of a familiar zoo creature (the first two stanzas establish a sense of familiarity and security), ends as a stunning vision. Muir seems right to have extolled the symbolic brilliance of this poem.

The key word 'mesmerized' — along with 'stares' and 'dream' — picks up the idea of a vision arriving and taking over consciousness, as in 'The Thought-Fox'. Again, these are no ordinary animals. In 'The Thought-Fox', the fox's predatory, imaginary power came as 'an eye'. Here, the jaguar may be 'blind', but it is the blindness of the visionary, who sees beyond his imprisoning surroundings, 'drills' through them even. The pulsating, driving rhythms of the poem, reinforced by heavy alliteration and assonance ('By the báng of bloód in the bráin déaf the éar'), help register an effect of barely suppressed rage, of potential violence.

Edwin Muir found in *The Hawk in the Rain* what he called an 'admirable violence'. The phrase is easily misunderstood, as is the presence of what it alludes to in Hughes's work. The jaguar's potential is clear enough — although you might compare this poem with its later companion piece, 'Second Glance at a Jaguar' (p. 72), in which the creature hurries along, 'Glancing sideways', as if 'looking for a target', but seems defeated. The meaning and effect of 'violence' in Hughes is not obvious. Even the title poem of Hughes's first collection, often taken as an indication of an excessive absorption in violence, reveals a position by no means so clear-cut. Let us look at it for a moment, and consider what it seems to be saying, and the means by which it does so. Is it violent? If so, in what sense?

The Hawk in the Rain

I drown in the drumming ploughland, I drag up
Heel after heel from the swallowing of the earth's mouth,
From clay that clutches my each step to the ankle
With the habit of the dogged grave, but the hawk

Effortlessly at height hangs his still eye.
His wings hold all creation in a weightless quiet,
Steady as a hallucination in the streaming air.
While banging wind kills these stubborn hedges,

Thumbs my eyes, throws my breath, tackles my heart,
And rain hacks my head to the bone, the hawk hangs
The diamond point of will that polestars
The sea drowner's endurance: and I,

Bloodily grabbed dazed last-moment-counting
Morsel in the earth's mouth, strain towards the master-
Fulcrum of violence where the hawk hangs still.
That maybe in his own time meets the weather

Coming the wrong way, suffers the air, hurled upside down,
Fall from his eye, the ponderous shires crash on him,
The horizon trap him; the round angelic eye
Smashed, mix his heart's blood with the mire of the land.

DISCUSSION

The very word 'violence' appears at the centre of this poem, as if to
cue us in to its subject. But it is not so much the violence of the
creature, the hawk, that it celebrates; rather, the violence inherent
in nature, which 'dogs' humanity, pulling us down to our earthly
graves. The poem seems to be about life as a condition of struggle
— a vain struggle to escape those elemental forces which, like the
weather, are always with us. (Compare with 'Wind', p. 28). It is an
astonishing, breathtaking enactment of power and energy,
hammering the reader with emphatic rhythms and strongly marked
alliterative stresses, from the dramatic opening ('I drówn in the
drúmming ploúghland, I drág up') to the dying fall at the end, as
'heart's blood' and 'mire' smash and mix. Physically violent verbs
('Thumbs my eyes, throws my breath, tackles my heart'), huge
adjectival phrases ('Bloodily grabbed dazed last-moment-counting')
and a free use of run-on-lines; all powerfully evoke the conflict

between being pulled down into the earth, and striving beyond it; between an ecstatic mastery and freedom, symbolised by the hawk hanging still, and a grim understanding of the inevitable, 'Coming the wrong way'. Only a hard, sharp ('diamond point') of will can momentarily sustain the wonderful illusion of stillness beyond time; then comes the death which has threatened from the start.

The point of the poem seems clear: we may feel we can choose when to die, but we cannot; we may feel we can evade nature, but we cannot. The ambiguity of 'hallucination' undermines the seemingly effortless stillness of the hawk, high up beyond the clutches of the earth, and prepares us for its end. All that driving rhetoric, the hyperbolic excess of statement, does perhaps eventually have a numbing effect (how can rain seem to hack one's head to the bone?). This may be why Hughes has excluded this poem from his *Selected Poems*. But the surprising strength and boldness of the conception remain, I believe: and it is easy to see that here, violence is the lesser theme. It is a form of uncontrolled energy which may give life or destroy it, depending upon the moment and nature of its appearance. The will to survive, a kind of unflinching stoicism in the face of mortality, emerges as the central meaning of the poem.

I will return to this issue of 'violence', which is unavoidable in any consideration of Hughes's work. But it is important to recognise at the outset the complexity of what's involved – a complexity apparent the moment specific, individual examples are looked at. There is the further point that, although when 'The Hawk in the Rain' and other poems in the collection first appeared, they hit the English poetic scene like a bombshell, this was as much the product of the prevailing trend towards self-effacing, detached, above all *safe* verse, as it was the result of Hughes's own striking originality. What Edwin Muir and others found in *The Hawk in the Rain* (and which was confirmed by its immediate successor, *Lupercal*, in 1960), was a clean break from the dominant trend of English poetry in the 'fifties, the quiet, domestic and sceptical verse of the so-called 'Movement'. The central Movement poem, Philip Larkin's 'At Grass' (1955), which was hugely popular, tapped the note of wistful regret, of nostalgia for lost greatness, which, it has been said, characterised the mood of the country at the time.[5] Hughes, whose 'A Dream of Horses' (from *Lupercal*) the influential critic A. Alvarez compared with Larkin's poem in the introduction to his anthology, *The New Poetry* (1962)) seemed to fulfil the demand for a new modern poetry which dropped the pretence that (in Alvarez' clumsy words) 'gentility, decency and all the other social totems will eventually muddle through'.[6] Larkin's poem was, according to Alvarez, *social*: his horses, seen standing anonymously cropping grass, bring with them images of 'Numbers and parasols ... The starting-gates, the crowds and cries'. Hughes, by contrast, imagines being a groom, whose night-time lantern's 'little orange flare' makes masks of his fellow-sleepers' dazed faces, faces that seem

> Bodiless, or else bodied by horses
> That whinnied and bit and cannoned the world from its place.

Unlike Larkin, Hughes wants to subvert the familiar, the everyday (significantly, he chooses a night setting), in order to take us back to an archaic realm of violent, impending possibilities:

> Now let us, tied, be quartered by these poor horses,
> If but doomsday's flames be great horses,
> The forever itself a circling of the hooves of horses.

Somewhat strained and awkwardly repetitive, 'A Dream of Horses' was also (with more justification than 'The Hawk in the Rain') excluded from the *Selected Poems*. Instead, Hughes chose another, earlier attempt to explore the impact of these creatures, called simply, 'The Horses' (pp. 19–20), which I would like to look at briefly. Not only does it seem to confirm Alvarez' view, implying once again the instinctual depths which lie beneath our passive, civilised selves; but it seems to do so with surprising control and delicacy. Do you agree?

DISCUSSION

'The Horses' focuses on the eruption of a dawn sun over the 'grey silent world' in which the horses stand mysterious and 'Megalith-still', the whole scene becoming like the 'fever of a dream' for the narrator. As before, Hughes resorts to dream to evoke the deeper feelings of strangeness and power which, he seems to be saying, lie awaiting resurrection within us.

But does it now seem as if I might have exaggerated the sense of power and energy created by his work, although it may be so surprising to a new reader? The quiet opening of 'The Horses' is *also* characteristic of Hughes:

I climbed through the woods in the hour-before-dawn dark.
Evil air, a frost-making stillness.

Not a leaf, not a bird,—
A world cast in frost. I came out above the wood.

Where my breath left tortuous statues in the iron light.

This finely-controlled, delicate simplicity is a feature of Hughes's
work far too often ignored. You might look too, at 'October Dawn'
(*SP*, p. 29), to see what I mean.

Nevertheless, I would suggest there is no doubt of the
immediate, battering-ram impact his first collection, dominated by
the title-poem, had; nor can there be little doubt that Hughes was
felt to be going his own way. What his contemporaries of the fifties
(such as Larkin, Donald Davie, Kingsley Amis, Vernon Scannell)
had in common, was

> the post-war mood of having had enough ... enough
> rhetoric, enough overweening push of any kind,
> enough of the dark gods, enough of the id, enough of
> the Angelic powers and the heroic efforts to make
> new worlds. They'd seen it all turn into death camps
> and atomic bombs. All they wanted was to get
> back into civvies and get home to the wife and kids
> and for the rest of their lives not a thing was going to
> interfere with a nice cigarette and a nice view of the
> park ... Now I came a bit later. I hadn't had enough. I was all for
> opening negotiations with whatever happened to be out there.[7]

It is helpful to see Hughes's poetry in this perspective, an
historical perspective – although the effect of his work is, as I aim to
show later, to deny history. His poems are designed to alert us to
another dimension of things, the dimension of 'dark gods' (an echo
of D. H. Lawrence), 'the id', 'Angelic powers' and 'heroic efforts'.
He wants to 'negotiate' with these forces, even if he is not, perhaps
cannot be, sure of what they are.

Hughes's sense of what lurks beneath the cosily domestic,
everyday surface of life is nowhere more powerfully conveyed than
in the remarkable poem 'Pike', published in *Lupercal*, his second
collection. To read 'Pike' is to recognise how it is that Hughes
quickly became, and remains, one of the most praised poets of his
generation. Can you see how the familiar, remembered experience
of a childhood pet is gradually deepened into a final, shocking
perception of horror and mystery at the heart of things? *How* is this

done, exactly? You might look particulary at the opening and
concluding stanzas (*SP*, pp. 59–60)

DISCUSSION

Some aspects of this poem should already be familiar to you now:
the striking opening impression; the rich, densely powerful imagery
unfolding with progressive inevitability towards that dramatic,
concluding moment; the strong, insistent, stress-based rhythms
reinforcing this onward movement, yet carefully restrained by the
four-line stanza structure. As before, Hughes binds his verses
tightly together by means of internal rhyme, alliteration and
assonance, concentrating especially on hard, plosive consonants to
add to the effect of suddenness and harshness in the phenomena
evoked – 'Pike in all parts, green tigering the gold. /Killers from the
egg: the malevolent aged grin.' By contrast with the brevity and
even violence with which we are encouraged to utter 'Pike', 'parts',
'egg' and 'grin', the drawn-out 'tigering' and 'malevolent'
encourage us to linger over their implications, so that the fish's
'dance' becomes a macabre celebration of timeless, instinctive
destructiveness. And this effect continues throughout the poem,
evoking sharp impressions of the immediate impact of the creature,
yet at the same time stirring up strange, atavistic memories of the
primitive horrors which rise towards the surface of consciousness in
the narrator.

  Interestingly, 'Pike', like 'The Thought-Fox', *has* a narrator,
although it is not at first apparent. Characteristically, the poem
begins with a series of evocative noun phrases, only indirectly (but
powerfully) suggestive of the subject-creature, without any
apparent observer. But there is one. We are made aware of this in
the fifth stanza ('Three we kept behind glass'), which suggests a
child or the young member of a household. 'Jungled' evokes a small
boy's or girl's impressions of a fish tank, at the same time adding a
new and limiting perspective to the opening impressions of
'submarine delicacy and horror'. This narrator goes on to give
further new dimensions to the poem, quietly measuring the fish as if
to contain them that way, but unable to avoid the memory of two
of 'six pounds each', dead in the willow-herb (a nicely English
rural-domestic touch), jammed into each other in the merciless
cannibalism of the species. Then, in what seems to be the third
section of this carefully structured poem (the stanzas fall into the
arrangement 4-3-4), the narrator, now 'I' – still struggling to resist
the full impact of those first impressions by noting prosaic details

such as that the pond is 'fifty yards across' — is forced to confront the mysterious reality which, like an 'eye', a 'dream' (familiar images now) comes swimming upwards. The 'legendary depth', as 'deep as England', in which the mysterious horror has its being, implies a more than personal perspective: suggesting that in our own present cosy corner of civilisation, with its quiet, domestic surface, there survive primitive forces whose evil otherness can only be dimly hinted at, but which — in the most disturbing, subversive aspect of the poem — are watching, waiting.

There is much more to be said about 'Pike', but this is some of what seems to me to be most important to the reader beginning to get to know Hughes's work. I've stressed its formal qualities, but only to reinforce the extent to which Hughes's evocation of an almost physical feeling of horror is, at its best, superbly controlled. 'Pike' also alerts us to the way in which his manner, like his matter, returns again and again, obsessively. And yet *Lupercal*, in which it appeared, can be seen as bringing to an end a phase in his work, his early phase. Fittingly, the concluding image of the book, from the title-poem, 'Lupercalia', begs:

> Maker of the world
> Hurrying the lit ghost of man
> Age to age while the body hold,
> Touch this frozen one.

The Lupercalia were Roman rituals in which fertility was supposed to be restored to barren women who were struck with whips by athletes racing through the streets. The divine energies of creativity remained at a distance from Ted Hughes for some years after this, until they re-emerged in *Wodwo*. Yet as we have seen, his work showed such persuasive and stunning force from the start that he quickly became one of the foremost poets in the language, widely recognised as an apparently unique interpreter of those lost, instinctual powers which, in poem after poem (e.g. also, 'Meeting', p. 27, 'Hawk Roosting', pp. 43–4 and 'Ghost Crabs', pp. 67–8) emerge out of a kind of dream to fix our attention.

3.   'Roots': the Poet and the Personal

I have been emphasizing the inward, personal dimension of Ted Hughes's poetry. This is not the same thing as saying that it is autobiographical. Nevertheless, there is an autobiographical tendency in his work which demands attention — attention which it is most appropriate to give in relation to some at least of what is known about his life so far. Hughes himself has observed that

> With the dynamo of any poet — any unusual poet — it is impossible to tell which is decisive, whether the peculiar forces of his time or his own peculiar make-up. One imagines that it is only those poets whose make-up somehow coincides with the vital impulse of their time who are able to come to real stature — when poets apparently more naturally gifted simply wither away. This was evidently enough the case with Shakespeare...[1]

Of course, Hughes does not have Shakespeare's stature. But he is one of our great poets. In this chapter I will explore something of what we know about his 'own peculiar make-up' in its relation to his poetry. How this might coincide with the 'vital impulse' of the time is much more difficult to define, and in any case rather beyond the scope of this book — although, as you will have noticed, I have already touched on Hughes's own sense of connection, or lack of it, with his contemporaries.

That Ted Hughes, as writer, is aware of the complexity of the whole issue is suggested by his remarks upon Shakespeare. It is also implied by a poem which he wrote (we happen to know) after a long gap of relative inactivity. It is 'Wodwo', the last poem of the volume to which it gave the title, *Wodwo*, published in 1967. Before turning to this poem (*SP.*, p. 114), it is worth mentioning that a 'wodwo' is something of a mystery-word, derived from one of Hughes's favourite poems, the anonymous fourteenth-century alliterative epic, *Sir Gawain and the Green Knight*, in which it is used, apparently (no one can be sure now) to describe a wild, half-human, half-animal creature met with in lonely places. Its aptness should become clear as you read the poem. While you do so, you might ask yourself how 'Wodwo' compares with the 'animal poems' you have read so far – 'The Jaguar', for example. In what way is this poem different? And do you see this difference having any bearing upon the question of the author's 'own peculiar make-up'? What do you make of the shape or structure of the poem, the absence of punctuation?

DISCUSSION

Perhaps the most obvious point is that 'Wodwo' is a more lighthearted, charming poem, than the fiercely energetic 'Jaguar'. It is at once quiet and obscure, like some snuffling little creature in the undergrowth; a somewhat sardonic little parable about looking for an identity ('What am I? it begins). The 'wodwo' lacks the awe-inspiring features of Hughes's earlier animals, his jaguar, fox or hawk; indeed, it lacks even the identity, 'animal', since it is self-questioning from the start. The whole point seems to be to leave us uncertain about the nature of its subject-narrator: whether it is human, or animal, or some mixture of both.

'Wodwo' also appears to be *shaped* in a rather unexpected, unusual way, doesn't it? We've seen in 'A Childish Prank' that Hughes went on to develop a much freer verse form after the tightly-controlled structures of 'The Thought-Fox' and similar poems. Here, after beginning within at least some of the familiar conventions of syntax and punctuation, the poem proceeds by losing even commas and full stops, the language itself becoming more questionable and uncertain, until finally even the capital letters which normally start lines and sentences are lost, and we are left with

> have I an owner what shape am I what
> shape am I am I huge if I go
>
> to the end on this way past these trees and past these trees

and so on, not knowing who it is or what it is, that supposes itself to be the centre of 'all this'. The remaining capitalised 'I' suggests only the persistence of the questing ego, confused and purposeless as it is. 'All this', it concludes, is 'very queer'. Yet, 'I'll go on looking'.

Hughes's earlier verse was still subject to the conventions of rhyme, stanza-pattern, clearly marked stress-rhythms, and syntax. Here he breaks into the much freer form of modern American poets such as Charles Olson, or William Carlos Williams, a form not very familiar to the English audience of the time. Of course, such verse is still shaped: in the appearance and order of words on the page, insubtle undercurrents of rhythm, emphasised by alliteration and assonance, in deceptively simple repetitions. Do you see what I mean? For example: 'tíll I get tíred that's tóuching óne wáll of me' ('get' and 'me' carrying, to my ear, a lighter emphasis). The exasperated movement of the searching 'wodwo' is recreated by the repetition of 'past these trees', as well as by the ironic reiteration in 'but there's all this what is it roots/roots roots roots', giving the feel of a creature rooting about — for its roots.

This is where the poem begins to make us think about the author's own make-up. Hughes appears to be questioning himself, and the kind of poetry he has been writing:

> Why do I find
> this frog so interesting as I inspect its most secret
> interior and make it my own?

Why indeed? Because the animal nature he has been capturing so brilliantly in his earlier, creaturely poems has served to explore his own nature and obsessions. Yet the self-assurance about this project which emanates from the first two collections, *The Hawk in the Rain* and *Lupercal*, which were published within a mere three years of each other (1957–60), has now, seven years later, become corroded, with the result that what he has to do now, all he can do now, is explore the 'very queer' nature of reality, is to 'go on looking'. Understanding this fundamental shift of approach and technique involves paying some attention to the personal or biographical perspective.

It may be that such a perspective can be related to the impulses of the time, when, as one historian has put it: 'the country, it seemed, was in a mess.'[2] But, again, this is far more difficult to ascertain. What we do know is that when *Wodwo* was finally published (1967), it elicited a mixture of enthusiasm and confusion from reviewers.[3] The tentativeness and uncertainty of the concluding, title-poem, seemed to pervade the entire volume, which contained an odd combination of poetry, prose and drama which, nevertheless, the author insisted in a 'Note', was 'intended to be read together, as parts of a single work.' Anyone reading the twenty-one poems, five short stories and radio play in *Wodwo* is likely to consider this special pleading on the author's part. Even Keith Sagar, Hughes's most comprehensive apologist, and the author of the first, full-length study of the poet's work, allows that *Wodwo* needs to be lived with 'for years' before it can be seen whole — hardly encouraging to the non-fanatic.[4] But there is material publicly available, which enables us at least to understand this development in Hughes's work, and which directs us to the personal struggle which underlies it.

It would be absurd to ignore the fact that in 1962 Hughes's marriage to the American poet Syivia Plath — from which had come two children — collapsed; followed by, a year later, Plath's suicide. A remarkable, and intensely productive partnership, had come to an abrupt and tragic end. It is possible to deal with this in a way which avoids idle speculation about the two poets' private lives. A prolific writer until these events took place, Hughes published no more than a handful of children's stories and poems — and some fugitive pieces in a limited edition called *Recklings* (1966), i.e., runts — during the following five years. *Meet my Folks!* (1961), the first of these books, contained a lively gallery of family portraits, along the lines of: 'Oh it would never do to let folks know/My sister's nothing but a great big crow.' In *The Earth-Owl and Other Moon People* (1963), charm turned to menace, as grotesque fantasy creatures such as the moon's 'hideous number nines' emerged, starting out of the ground 'with such a shout/The chosen victim's eyes instantly fall out.' *How the Whale Became* (1963), his first prose work for children, revealed a milder, more free-wheeling inventiveness, reminiscent of Kipling's *Just So Stories* (1902). It was immediately followed by the slight, but likeable, lolloping verse-drama, *Nessie the Mannerless Monster* (1963), a creature who marched south into Yorkshire to find the streets 'all empty and bare' because everybody 'sits indoors in front/of the T.V. with a dead stare.' The impression of a powerful poetic imagination barely turning over is everywhere apparent in these minor works — not minor because they are for children, but because of the quality of what is in them. You need only glance at one of Hughes's later books for children, such as *The Iron Man* (1968), a rich and gripping little prose-epic about a metal-eating creature who appears out of nowhere and ends up saving the world from a space-monster, to recognise that the weakness of his earlier children's books has nothing to do with the genre. Moreover, the horror

which frequently surfaces in them is barely controlled — a feeling
you might care to confirm by glancing over some poems written in
1963 but not published until *Wodwo*: 'Ghost Crabs', 'Gog', 'The
Rat's Dance' and 'The Howling of Wolves' (*SP*, pp. 67–8, 93, 100,
109). (I will return to 'Ghost Crabs'.)

What, then, had happened? Sylvia Plath was born 27 October
1932 in Boston, Massachusetts, of Austrian and German parents,
and lived in America until she won a Fulbright scholarship to
Cambridge in 1955, where she met Ted Hughes, whom she married
in June 1956. Hughes, a Yorkshireman, had gone up to Cambridge
in 1951 to read English, after two years National Service in the
RAF, mostly spent on a remote radio station, reading and rereading
Shakespeare and watching the grass grow.[5] He had switched to
Archaeology and Anthropology before graduating in 1954. Thereaf-
ter he did some school teaching and took various odd jobs, including
working in a zoo, before meeting his wife. Sylvia Plath
had had a brilliant academic career before coming to England, but
had already shown signs of serious mental disturbance, including
one suicide attempt (later described in her novel *The Bell Jar*,
1963). Hughes had published little, she had published more; neither
had displayed very much sign of what was to come. Then Sylvia
Plath began to submit Hughes's poems to magazines in ever-
increasing numbers, until finally she entered his work for an
American competition for a first book of poems — which he won
with what became *The Hawk in the Rain*. At the same time, Plath
had several of her own poems accepted by the prestigious Chicago
magazine *Poetry*. From 1957 to 1959, the two lived in the United
States in an intensely creative partnership, reading and criticising
each other's work. They taught at first, but then began to write
full-time, before returing to England to settle. After a few weeks
with Hughes's family at Heptonstall in Yorkshire, they took a small
flat in London, where their first child Frieda was born in April
1960. The following summer they moved to Devon, where Hughes
now lives. There Nicholas Farrar Hughes was born in January
1962. Their marriage soon showed signs of strain, and Hughes left
his wife for another woman. Plath began divorce proceedings and,
unwilling to face another winter in the country, returned to London
with her children. There she found herself in a flat on her own
during the worst winter for fifty years. Ill and depressed, she killed
herself on 11 February 1963.

Inevitably, there is a strong temptation to link the poetry of Ted
Hughes and Sylvia Plath, which shares an extremism, an insistence
on facing the worst. But it is a temptation to be resisted since, as
Plath herself remarked, 'we write poems that are as distinct and

different as our fingerprints themselves must be.'[6] More important
here is the link between what happened to Plath and its effect upon
the development of Hughes's poetry, not only interrupted by the
personal tragedies in which he was involved (in March 1969 his
companion Assia Gutsmann and her child Shura died as Plath had
done before them) but profoundly darkened as a result. It is hard
not to feel that the cumulative impact of these events lies behind the
emergence of that terrible vision which dominates the *Crow*
sequence, first published in 1970, and dedicated to the memory of
'Assia and Shura'.

Yet Hughes is not, like Plath and some of her American mentors
(such as Robert Lowell), a 'confessional' poet, tracing his own life
and circumstances explicitly in his work. That is not the nature of
the connection. Even the opening sequence of *Moortown* (1979), a
verse journal of Hughes's experiences working with Jack Orchard,
who became his father-in-law in 1970 after he married Orchard's
daughter Carol — even these poems are more notable for the detailed
intensity with which natural processes and farm activities are
depicted, than for any directly personal revelations. Consider, for
example, 'Now You Have to Push' (p. 198), one of these
'Moortown Elegies', as Hughes first called them. How personal
would you say it is? What features of it make you think of it as
personal, and what is its overall tone?

DISCUSSION

I would say that this poem seems both personal and impersonal:
personal, because of the directness of address (specifically
expressed in terms of the repeated use of 'you' and 'your') and the
affectionately detailed description of the addressee ('Your careful
little moustache'); impersonal, because of the quiet, calm tone in
which the simple but profound sense of loss is conveyed:

> The trustful cattle, with frost on their backs,
> Waiting for hay, waiting for warmth,
> Stand in a new emptiness.

The directly personal relationship is not mentioned, or even
touched on, although it lay behind the choice of subject.

The overall mood of the 'Moortown Elegies' is one of calm
acceptance, as if Hughes finally found something he had been
looking for, through his earlier, dark and turbulent work — his

own roots, perhaps? But what, exactly, are those roots? We need to go back a little. Sylvia Plath's first impression was revealing: 'I met the strongest man in the world', she enthused to her mother from Cambridge in 1956, 'ex-Cambridge, brilliant poet whose work I loved before I met him, a large, hulking, healthy Adam, half French, half Irish, with a voice like the thunder of God — a singer, story-teller, lion and world-wanderer ...'[7] Hughes *is* a large man ('Am I huge', the narrator of 'Wodwo' enquires, playing upon the sound and shape of its creator and his name); and he undoubtedly has a remarkable poetic and story-telling gift. But his origins are somewhat less exotic, as he himself revealed in some autobiographical remarks in *Poetry in the Making* (1967), a book based on a series of radio talks for schools which engaged him during the period shortly after his first wife's death.

'My interest in animals', he confessed there, 'began when I began'[8] He began on 17 August 1930, as Edward James Hughes, the son of a carpenter and the youngest of three children, in Mytholmroyd, a small town west of Halifax in the West Riding of Yorkshire. His earliest memories reflect an abiding fascination with the creaturely world: memories of an indoors toy zoo, of hunting and fishing with his brother (who later became a gamekeeper), of scrambling about the hills. When he was seven, the family moved to Mexborough, a small coalmining town in south Yorkshire, where his parents ran a tobacconist and newsagent's shop, and where he attended the local grammar school. His friends were town boys, sons of colliers and railway men, with whom he led 'one life, but all the time I was leading this other life in the country', searching for and trapping animals. It was a dual existence: 'civilised' life on one side, 'nature', especially animal nature, on the other. At about fifteen 'my life grew more complicated and my attitude to animals changed. I accused myself of disturbing their lives. I began to look at them, you see, from their own point of view'.[9] At the same time, he began to write his first poems — not animal poems, that came later; but typically boyish adventure tales about Zulus and the Wild West.

Yet before he left school, Hughes could write this:

O lady, consider when I shall have lost you
The moon's full hands, scattering waste,
The sea's hands, dark from the world's breast,
The world's decay where the wind's hands have passed,
And my head, worn out with love, at rest,
In my hands, and my hands full of dust,
O my lady.

'Song', his first published poem (reprinted in full in *SP*, p. 14), reveals the powerful effect upon Hughes of a book he was given by a sympathetic English master: Robert Graves's *The White Goddess* (first published 1946), probably the single most important influence upon his thought and work. Graves's book is a fascinating, obsessive reworking of Biblical, Celtic and Greek mythology (and much else besides) into an 'historical grammar' of the 'active principles of poetic myth', based on the assumption that the dominance of rational thought in Europe since Socrates has all but destroyed the magical, religious and truthful understanding of life, and our relationship with nature, vouchsafed the ancient bards. 'The function of poetry is religious invocation of the Muse', according to Graves; 'its use is the experience of mixed exaltation and horror that her presence excites'. This muse is the lunar muse Hughes's 'Song' tries to capture, in some of her various manifestations — cold and distant mother of the gods, warm and intimate creator of mankind. 'The poet is in love with the White Goddess, with Truth: his heart breaks with longing and love for her', writes Graves. Her 'unseen presence' can be felt in all the elements, yet it is a presence ignored nowadays, when 'serpent, lion and eagle belong to the circus-tent; ox, salmon and boar to the cannery; racehorse and greyhound to the betting ring; and the sacred grove to the sawmill'; even the moon is 'despised as a burnt-out satellite'. Graves sees himself as 'the fox who has lost his brush'.[10]

Hughes's prompt and lasting interest in *The White Goddess* is immediately comprehensible to any reader of his work: he is evidently just as deeply committed to a vision of our troubled relationship with nature, a relationship he similarly imagines in terms of animal imagery and symbolism drawn from the vast storehouse of European mythology; he also has an exalted conception of the poet's role in society, which has, finally, led him to accept what might otherwise seem a surprising position — that of Laureate. He feels that by exploring his own imagination, he is exploring everyone's; he is the poet as bard, as singer of the community's songs, expressing itself to itself, defining its real identity.

This view gives a peculiar significance to his own make-up, turning even the mundane facts of his background into material worthy of poetic expression. Hence, for example, his interest in the possibility that his mother, Edith Farrar, may have been descended from Nicholas Ferrar, founder of the Anglican community at Little Gidding which is celebrated in T. S. Eliot's *Four Quartets* – a possibility which led to a poem on Ferrar (in *Lupercal*), as well as the name of his son. Edith Hughes may also have been descended from the seventeenth century bishop Robert Farrar, whose martyrdom Hughes describes in a grisly little poem (*SP*, pp. 33–4). But it was Hughes's father William's appalling World War One experiences which touched him more deeply, and led to a continuous theme in his work: the memory of war. This memory, of a war he himself never knew, seems to have become interwoven with the memory of his birth-place, the intense gloominess of which has led him to say, 'I can never lose the impression that the whole region is in mourning for the first world war.'[11] Anyone familiar with small rural communities still dominated by their war memorials knows what this means: war is as near as the personal memories which remain of all those who left these communities, never to return. Hughes's mythologising tendency does not altogether obscure this, although, as we shall see in chapter 4, only a small number of poems confront the memory of war directly.

Mytholmroyd, where the Hughes family lived in an end terrace house backing on to a canal, is a few miles from Haworth, home of the Brontës a hundred years before. As with other features of his home and family, this fact plays its part in what he chooses to write about. Like Haworth, Mytholmroyd is situated in the valley of the upper Calder, between moor and factory; like Haworth, it feels on the edge of civilisation, close to elemental nature — a feeling which, interwoven with the history of the place, Hughes has celebrated in a number of poems in *Remains of Elmet* (1979), including 'Haworth Parsonage', 'Top Withins' and 'Emily Brontë'.

Please now read 'Emily Brontë' (reprinted in *Selected Poems* (p. 179)), and note how Hughes locates the specific, natural and historic associations of his home environment within his poetry, as part of a familiar drama. It is very telling, is it not? Precisely because of its known associations. Just compare it with, for example, 'Wind' (p. 28): the perspective has shifted, hasn't it? The elemental power of nature continues to inspire the poet, but in 'Emily Brontë' it is nature located, and humanised, by its explicit connection with an actual person.

Many of the poems in *Remains of Elmet* are about actual people, including members of Hughes's own family. The volume is dedicated to his mother, and opens with a prefatory poem to his uncle. It seems as if when Hughes turns to his roots, his own personal connection with the landscape and its associations humanises his vision. According to a note in *Remains of Elmet*, the valley of the upper Calder was once part of the ancient Kingdom of Elmet, 'last ditch' of the native Celts before the invading Angles, and for centuries an 'uninhabitable wilderness' which, in the early

1800s, became the centre of the textile industry; since then, however, the mills and 'their attendant chapels' have died, the whole landscape and its people, 'so rooted for so long ... changing rapidly'. It is in response to this sense of loss that Hughes memorialises his landscape and its people.

What he chooses to remember, however, isn't always favourably depicted. Look for a moment at 'Mount Zion' (pp. 169–170). What do you make of this evidently personal poem? How successfully does Hughes convey this aspect of his roots? Is the effect at all undermined by phrases such as 'convulsed Moses' mouthings'? (Note 'Mount Zion' is a common name for evangelical chapels, derived from the Old Testament notion of the place to which the elect of God have already come. Hence too, the reference to 'Wesley's foundation stone' in the third stanza: in the village of Heptonstall, above Mytholmroyd, there is, it is claimed, the oldest continuously-used Methodist chapel in the world.)

DISCUSSION

It is easy to see that the poem *is* personal, the repeated stress upon the personal pronoun, without any hint that this might be a dramatised persona: '*my* birth moon', '*I* knew what was coming', 'They terrified *me*', culminating in that telling image of the young boy 'smothered in bed', where he could hear

> them
> Riving at the religious stonework
> With screwdrivers and chisels.

'They' are trying to get at the cricket which, singing from a crack in the chapel wall, is undermining the self-denying, joyless puritanism of the whole Calder valley. What Hughes elsewhere calls the 'iron arteries of Calvin' ('Warriers of the North', SP, p. 99), run through his memories of home, the very landscape of his upbringing, and help explain further the frightening presence, the eye which often comes 'slowly towards me, watching' ('Pike', p. 60).

But this attempt to mock 'Mount Zion' does not quite come off, does it? There is an element of exaggeration, of rhetorical overkill, which unbalances the poem, isn't there? An indictment expressed in terms of 'convulsed Moses' mouthings' — an awkward, clumsy phrase — is bound to falter, if not fail. And why does Hughes allow this to happen? Perhaps because he cannot ever escape the dark, oppressive atmosphere associated with his childhood valley —

whether because of the memory of war; or Mount Zion's 'gravestone slab' blocking his 'birth moon'; or the massive shadow of Scout Rock which, he says, shut his home off from the rest of the world and seemed to hang over him, having 'watched' him from 'my first day'.[12] All this seems to have shaped Hughes's view of life. In 'Crag Jack's Apostasy' (in *Lupercal*), he uses the persona of 'Crag Jack' (his grandfather) to explore the possibility of 'coming clear' of 'all the dark churches' that 'Stooped over my cradle once' by imagining the arrival of a dream-animal, a wolf. Again, it is the fearful, dark quality of the alternative to his childhood 'churches' which is most notable. In the directly autobiographical story, 'Sunday', in *Wodwo*, he tells of a young boy's frustration amidst the stifling sabbatarianism of his home village, a frustration only relieved by a daydream-wolf, then by the strange sight of 'Billy Red', who kills rats with his teeth — the forerunner of the tramps and outcasts he occasionally celebrates for their closeness to the elemental (e.g. 'November', pp. 51–2).

However it may arrive, the primal force of nature is what Hughes seems to feel has been suppressed or denied, and it is this which his personal experience recalls again and again. The force of nature is present in history; but Hughes imagines it as part of an ancient, dim and bloody past which our rational-Christian civilisation has 'forgotten'. It may appear rooted in the cosily domestic and familiar, but, he also wishes to suggest, it goes back beyond any known or imagined personal history. Look, for instance, at 'Thistles', again from *Wodwo* (see *SP*, p. 63). What is it about? And what is its tone? How does it compare with 'Mount Zion'?

DISCUSSION

Like those poems which are about animals, but also about much more, so too, does this tell us about the familiar plants of its title, but also much more than that. The 'rubber tongues' of the cows which lick them, and the 'hoeing hands' of men which disturb them, make the thistles seem cosily domestic, even innocent; but, typically, Hughes's vision transforms them into 'a grasped fistful/Of splintered weapons and Icelandic frost', as the archaic, repressed memory of Viking invaders 'Stiff with weapons, fighting back over the same ground', looms into focus. This is what, apparently, lies beneath the everyday surface of life: a vengeful reality which demands to be remembered.

The tone of 'Thistles' is exaggerated, but it is not the exaggeration of 'Mount Zion', is it? Rather, it is gently absurd, drawing a contrast between these unprepossessing plants and the battling warriors which is as comic as it is surprising. Without such humour, Hughes's endorsement of the dark elementals can seem excessive — as in 'Thrushes' (p. 57), which he imagines having a 'bullet and automatic purpose' in their 'bounce and stab' for worms like (how can we believe it?) 'Mozart's brain' or 'the shark's mouth'. Another way of putting this is to say that when Hughes can be detached about the personal, he is capable of humour, with persuasive and enjoyable results. A good example is provided by the very beautiful and relaxed little poem about his daughter in *Wodwo*, called 'Full Moon and Little Frieda' (p. 113). It offers a scene of tender, amused contemplation:

> A cool small evening shrunk to a dog bark and the clank of a
> bucket —
>
> ...
>
> "Moon!" you cry suddenly, "Moon! Moon!"
>
> The moon has stepped back like an artist gazing amazed at a
> work
>
> That points at him amazed.

Do we need to know who 'Little Frieda' is? In such a poem, Hughes's 'roots' do not tug us back towards themselves. (You might also compare it with 'You Hated Spain', evidently addressed to Sylvia Plath, *SP* pp. 135–6).

I have been trying to expose Hughes's 'roots' as a means of understanding how he presents himself and his background in certain of his poems; and also to suggest some aspects of how his life and his work might be interrelated. This is, as I hope you will have realised by now, a complex matter, involving interpretation and judgement — of the 'facts', as of the poems. While it would be an obvious mistake to assume that any of Hughes's poems are simply forms of personal expression, it is helpful to read some of them in the light of what is known about his life, not only to explain obscure or puzzling allusions (as in 'Mount Zion' and 'Wodwo'), but also to get to grips with the problem of the 'personal' in this poet's work.

4. The Memory of War

I have suggested that Hughes is rather an obsessive poet, returning
again and again to certain themes. This is most obvious in his
continued and continuing exploration of natural, and especially
animal imagery, symbolism and myth. No wonder, then, that he is
so often labelled an 'animal poet'. But he could almost as well have
been labelled a 'war poet'. Not quite in the same sense as, say,
Wilfred Owen (1893–1918), who wrote directly out of his
experiences in the trenches of the First World War, and whose
poetry has influenced Hughes; nor, perhaps, in the same sense as
another 'active service' poet, Keith Douglas (1920–44), who wrote
out of his experiences in the Western Desert during the Second
World War, and whose poetry Hughes has helped promote. Rather,
he is a war poet at one remove, writing out of the impact of memory
— the individual memory of his father, and the collective memory of
English culture.

You have only to open the first page of a recent collection,
Flowers and Insects (1986), to find the sound and movement of
some innocent narcissi associated with

> a rustling, silent film
> Of speeded-up dancing
> And laughing children
> From the 1918 Armistice.
>
> ('Narcissi')

What, we ask ourselves, is an old newsreel of 'the 1918 Armistice'
doing in a contemporary poem about flowers? It is more than a

question of surprise — although that effect is important. What might have been an easy, sentimental image of flowers rustling and dancing like happy children is, instead, an almost shocking suggestion of how such happy, peaceful images carry inexorably with them the dark memories of this century.

To anyone familiar at all with Hughes's work and perhaps, his background too, any surprise occasioned by the apparently arbitrary entry of the First World War into an innocent 'nature poem' is quickly modified: by the realisation that, in no other contemporary poet is the memory of war, particularly the First World War, so abidingly present. Two of his earliest published poems were 'The Jaguar' (which we have already looked at), and 'The Casualty', which is about a dead airman in an English village field. His first published collection, *The Hawk in the Rain*, opened with five 'animal' poems, including 'The Jaguar', but this was out of a total of forty, of which the concluding six were explicitly 'war' poems, including 'The Casualty'. Most of the poems retained for his *Selected Poems* were taken from these two groups, the 'animal' poems and the 'war' poems. We've looked at several 'animal' poems; now I would like to consider some of the 'war' poems — but also poems in which (like 'Narcissi') war may not be the ostensible subject, yet its presence as a central or shaping metaphor is important. Inevitably, our discussion will touch once again upon the problem of Hughes's 'violence'.

Let us begin immediately by looking at one of the poems Hughes selected from *The Hawk in the Rain*, 'Six Young Men' (pp. 31–2). How does the poet handle the war theme here? Does the poem go beyond the specific war in which these young men were killed? Remembering what was said in the preceding chapter about the poet's early background, do you find any significance in the time and place alluded to in this poem? It is, is it not, an ambivalent poem — can you see wherein the ambivalence lies? What do you make of the use of the word 'exposure' in particular?

DISCUSSION

The poem is not *directly* about war, is it? Yet, obviously, it calls upon several familiar images of the war experience: one 'lay/Calling in the wire', another was 'potting at tin-cans in no-man's land' when he was shot. But these are *memories*, aren't they? This poem is about the impact of war upon those who remain; in particular, the narrator and those he addresses so intimately. It explores the mixed feelings generated by the photograph which has immortalised the forty-years dead. It is about the memory of war; and the ambivalence of that memory.

Ambivalence is suggested by the way the poet handles the war theme, from the opening image of a 'faded and ochre-tinged' picture which, despite these marks of time, shows six young men with hands and faces unwrinkled, to the powerful, dramatic climax in which we are invited to realise

> That man's not more alive whom you confront
> And shake by the hand, see hale, hear speak loud,
> Than any of these six celluloid smiles are,
> Nor prehistoric or fabulous beast more dead...

Life and death co-exist as the longer-term memory is brought up short by the immediate memory of meeting a friend. The men's mortality has been repeatedly stressed, each of the first four stanzas concluding with a (cumulative) reminder that they are indeed 'dead', 'under the ground', then 'killed', then 'rotting'. The sudden turn towards the imaginary addressee in the last stanza, exploits our own sense of being alive, our predictable reaction to all this talk about death, and invites us to share the possibility that looking at this photograph 'might well dement'. Why might it? Presumably because, if we have responded fully to the immediacy of the poem's 'exposure' of death, we feel for an instant as if that is more vivid, the dead more alive, than ourselves in our own lives today. The word 'exposure' focuses the ambivalences, the 'contradictory permanent horrors' of the poem: it involves a profoundly ironic pun, whereby the killing 'flash' of a battlefield explosion (stanza 4) has been anticipated by the small glare of a photographer's light-bulb. We, too, are thereby exposed, by seeing the fixed smiles of the six young men all long dead, to an experience which will 'shoulder out' in a brutally physical way our own present sensations of being alive.

So the poem is about becoming aware of death through the reminder of war — not just any war, a specific war. We can easily tell which one: 'four decades' is quite explicit (the poem was first published in 1957), like the other details which connect the poem to a personal time and place, perhaps most effectively in the elegiac stanza 2:

> ... I know
>
> That bilberried bank, that thick tree, that black wall
> Which are there yet and not changed. From where these sit

> You hear the water of seven streams fall
> To the roarer in the bottom, and through all
> The leafy valley a rumouring of air go.

After the stark series of statements introduced by 'I know', we are drawn into a brilliantly metamorphosed image of the sound of a waterfall becoming like the sound of a whole community murmuring about themselves ('rumouring'). And we know now which community it is: Hughes's own, in the Calder Valley, of West Yorkshire, resounding with that memory of the First World War which seems to Hughes to hang over the place still. The photograph which is the subject of 'Six Young Men' belonged to his father, a picture of young comrades-in-arms, as they were to become, out on a Sunday jaunt, so very much alive and unaware that they were shortly to die.

This is how personal memory has entered the poet's experience; a family, and a community memory which is as alive as those who continue to live with it. When poet-critic Alan Bold visited Bill Hughes in his house in Heptonstall Slack in July 1974, the old man

> began to talk about the war. He began by shaking his head and saying 'it were a rough do' and went on to produce his Smallbook which had been so packed with Yorkshire mementoes that it had stopped a piece of shrapnel.[1]

Hughes's father had been a sergeant with the Lancashire Fusiliers, and one of seventeen men from his entire regiment (i.e., about 2%) to return from the disastrous landings at Gallipoli in 1915. According to his son's testimony, his terrible war experiences, a 'four-year mastication by gunfire and mud', were repeatedly transmitted to the young boy, lying 'small and four' on the domestic carpet, his father's 'luckless double' because

> His memory's buried, immovable anchor,
> Among jaw-bones and blown-off boots, tree-stumps,
>   shell-cases and craters ...
>   ('Out', *SP*, p. 95)

These fragments litter Hughes's work, as battle dominates his imagination. Poetry, for him, is 'for life in a world where people actually do die'; what excites his imagination 'is the war between vitality and death, and my poems may be said to celebrate the exploits of the warriors of either side'. In each of his poems, 'beside the principal subject ... there is what is not so easy to talk about,

Bodies on the battlefield, Western Front

even generally, but which is the living and individual element ... [it] brings to peace all the feelings and energies which, from all over the body, heart, and brain, send their champions onto the battle-ground of the first subject.'[2]

It has been suggested[3] that a whole generation of modern English poets have similarly experienced the First World War at one remove, through their parents' memories, which hover behind, for example, Philip Larkin's 'MCMXIV', or Vernon Scannell's 'The Great War' and 'Remembrance Day' — all written, like Hughes's poems, after the *Second* World War. This is perhaps less surprising when you consider how deep and lasting the effect of the so-called Great War has been on the consciousness of the British and, indeed, the people of Europe as a whole. The First World War was the first war of a fully industrialised economy, of mass conscription; it ushered in the age in which we live, an age in which the remorseless, overwhelming impact of technology and mass society has become a fact of all our lives. That war also signalled the end of nineteenth century notions of inevitable material and spiritual progress. Gallipoli and the Somme brought killing on a much wider, more mechanised scale than ever before. Even though those battles may nowadays seem old-fashioned, it may be that, as the military histo-rian John Keegan has pointed out, the remembered experiences of that war continue to hold contemporary writers and their audiences because we recognize that from them we have learnt as much as we ever will about what modern wars can do to men. We have perceived that some limit to what human beings can stand and cannot stand on the battle field has 'at last been reached; that none of the refinements of military technique of perfection of weapons achieved by science since 1918 [has] effectively worsened the pre-dicament of the individual' in the 'killing zone'; and that 'the voice from the trenches' speaks 'for every soldier of the industrial age.'[4] For many, including Hughes, the battles of the First World War, as they are remembered, seem to have become essential metaphors for the experience of war and, by extension, for life in the face of death.

In the long poem 'Out' (which means abroad in arms), from *Wodwo*, the derivation of Hughes's awareness of war is explained by the opening section, in which his enforced participation in his father's remembered experiences is like a dream imposed upon his childish consciousness, destroying his innocence. As so often in Hughes, this dream apparently offers a stronger sense of reality than reality itself, which is here the cosy domestic hearth of the Hughes' home. In part II (pp. 95—6), the poet goes on to imagine birth as no more than the production of cannon-fodder, a

nightmare vision of 'reassembled' infantry men tottering out of the
womb. Part III, 'Remembrance Day' (pp. 96–7), develops the idea
of the inextricability of birth and death under the shadow of the
memory of war, and yet also suggests a struggle to escape, doesn't
it? The remembrance day poppy is like a wound with its open
redness, a mouth, the mouth of a grave, the womb ...

It is years since I wore one.

It is more years
The shrapnel that shattered my father's paybook

Gripped me, and all his dead
Gripped him

But now,

goodbye to that bloody-minded flower.
You dead bury your dead.
Goodbye to the cenotaphs on my mother's breasts.

Goodbye to all the remaindered charms of my father's survival.
(pp. 96–7)

Ironically echoing the title of Robert Graves's First World War
autobiography, *Goodbye To All That* (1929), Hughes tries to
exorcise his memories, the memories of a war experienced by his
parents. However, he cannot. The grip of the past is too persistent;
it has become part of how he sees the present.

This helps us to understand all those poems in which the
remembered war seems more intense than life today. In 'The
Casualty', the sudden arrival of the dead and burning airman
confronts the farmers in their fields, the housewives 'behind
steamed windows', with a reality which 'Bulks closer greater flesh
and blood than their own.' The unignorable intrusion of war in the
person of this dead man makes him seem momentarily more alive
than the living, who are 'helpless as ghosts' at his funeral pyre. This
is similar to the concluding point made by 'Six Young Men',
although more sensationally expressed. Yet 'The Casualty' also
suggests an awareness of the dubious, voyeuristic potential of this
subject: the onlookers want to enter the burning airman's
experience, 'Greedy to share all that is undergone.'[5] Hughes, too,
wants to identify with soldiers at the moment of death, and we also
are invited to do so: in 'Bayonet Charge', for instance, which opens
dramatically with 'Suddenly he awoke and was running' (p. 30).
Look also at 'Bowled Over' (p. 75). But, how far are we to enjoy —

if that is the right word — this kind of experience, and how far
remain detached?

At least we can say, I think, that Hughes does not betray
himself, or the memories he is exploiting, by promoting what Owen
called 'The old Lie: Dulce et decorum est/Pro patria mori' ('Dulce et
Decorum Est', written 1917). 'Desertion in the face of a bullet!' is
what, sarcastically, Hughes calls death in battle, which quickly
cancels out 'King, honour, human dignity, etcetera' (pp. 75 and
30). Indeed, past and present butcheries seem all too alike for any
indulgence in patriotic sentimentalities: they coalesce into a single
appalling image of all those marching soldiers who haunt our
civilisation, who get

> their bravery
> From the dead millions of ghosts
> Marching in their boots, cumbering their bodies,
> Staring from under their brows, concentrating
> Toward a repeat performance.

This is from the opening section of 'Scapegoats and Rabies', a
group of five poems first published as a pamphlet in 1967, before
they appeared in the American edition of *Wodwo*, along with
several 'war' poems and a short radio play about a soldier with a bad
head wound. Significantly, Hughes included the whole of
'Scapegoats' in *Selected Poems* (pp. 82–7). If you read the opening
section, entitled 'A Haunting' (pp. 82–3), you will, I think, see how
war is understood to be a permanent aspect of our civilisation — a
fact which the poet notes with pity and anger, not joy. It is this
pervasive awareness of war which has, I believe, generated the
darkly pessimistic outlook of Hughes's poetry — war not only as an
ostensible   subject,   but   as   a   characteristic   metaphoric
transformation of a wide range of subjects.

Consider 'Mayday on Holderness', for example (pp. 35–6). Can
you see where the memory of the First World War suddenly
emerges? What effect does this have upon your overall impression
of the poem?

DISCUSSION

The memory of war clearly emerges in the penultimate stanza,
doesn't it? — in which, beneath the 'soundless' North Sea,

> Smoulder the wars: to heart-beats, bomb, bayonet.
> "Mother, Mother!" cries the pierced helmet.
> Cordite oozings of Gallipoli ...

The poet's specific, personal memory reappears suddenly, as a disrupting, subterranean set of now familiar images disrupting the initial, overall impression of domestic comfort and security, the 'motherly summer' day, the couples 'laughing in the lanes', where the owl announces its 'sanity' and the very stars seem to make 'pietas'. But I wonder if this does not happen in too arbitrary, *because* so personal, a manner? Are not the 'Cordite oozings of Gallipoli' rather too vague a gesture to transform the personal memory into one we can share?

Perhaps the problem is that in 'Mayday on Holderness' the memory of war is only partially transformed. To explain what I mean, I would draw your attention to a poem which accompanied 'Mayday on Holderness' in *Lupercal*, but which has not been reprinted in *Selected Poems*. It is worth considering in full, so I have included it below. Please now read it, asking yourself, firstly, how the memory of war may be felt in it; and, secondly, what attitude(s) we are invited to take up towards war, and violence in general. You might also think about how it compares with 'Pike', which we looked at earlier.

To Paint a Water Lily

A green level of lily leaves
Roofs the pond's chamber and paves

The flies' furious arena: study
These, the two minds of this lady.

First observe the air's dragonfly
That eats meat, that bullets by

Or stands in space to take aim;
Others as dangerous comb the hum

Under the trees. There are battle-shouts
And death-cries everywhere hereabouts

But inaudible, so the eyes praise
To see the colours of these flies

Rainbow their arcs, spark, or settle
Cooling like beads of molten metal

Through the spectrum. Think what worse
Is the pond-bed's matter of course;

Prehistoric bedragonned times
Crawl that darkness with Latin names,

Have evolved no improvements there,
Jaws for heads, the set stare,

Ignorant of age as of hour —
Now paint the long-necked lily-flower

Which, deep in both worlds, can be still
As a painting, trembling hardly at all

Though the dragonfly alight,
Whatever horror nudge her root.

DISCUSSION

Do you agree that this a more successful poem than 'Mayday on Holderness'? It evokes quite contrary feelings: of, on the one hand, quiet, detached, 'aesthetic' comtemplation, as we are invited to observe the delicately beautiful, pastoral-domestic setting of the lily; and, on the other, of violent, instinctual dread, as we are also invited to consider the

> battle-shouts

And death-cries everywhere hereabouts

But inaudible

The memory of war is brought in by means of these powerful, hyperbolic metaphors, violently transforming the familiar hum and buzz of an ordinary English country garden pond, where even the innocent dragon fly seems to 'bullet by', or 'stands in space to take aim'. As in the 'stilled legendary depth' of the pond in 'Pike', there is here once again an unnameable horror approaching from below, primitive, strange, rising to the surface of consciousness. Yet, unlike 'Pike', this poem does not, I think, leave us with the fear of being invaded by that atavistic, brutal realm; rather, it is kept at a distance, a separate world, which may make us tremble, like the lily nudged by 'horror', but which leaves us 'still', as a painting, a still-life might leave us. Art, the poem implies, controls and distances, even as it hints at what lurks beneath our everyday awareness of things.

This attitude is forcefully confirmed by the poem's remarkable, tense structure: a highly controlled and controlling series of thirteen octosyllabic couplets, half-rhyming, within which Hughes deploys

his familiar, hammering alliterative rhythms, four beats to the line
('That eáts méat, that búllets bý'), so punching home each set of
linking images. These strong rhythms themselves go back very far, as
far as the 'Prehistoric bedragonned times' the poet invokes: the
Anglo-Saxon epic *Beowulf* may not be prehistoric, but it deals in
dragons, derives from at least the eighth century AD and there can
be little doubt that, consciously or not, Hughes is hearking back to
that old heroic Anglo-Saxon verse form, the four-beat alliterative
line. Just as a poem like 'To Paint a Water Lily' emphasises the
submerged violence of long ago, so, too, it adapts the forms of an
earlier poetry, as 'primitive' as its subject. Elsewhere, in 'Famous
Poet' (*SP*, pp. 16–7), Hughes attacks the mouse-like demeanour of
poets who, he claims, lack the 'vital fire' poetry needs, are unable to
recreate the 'old heroic bang'. It is a 'bang' which echoes clearly
enough through his own work, if not always in terms of battering
rhythms, then at least in the recurring emphasis upon the sounds of
warfare.

Poems such as 'To Paint A Water Lily' attempt to make us aware of
the threat of violence and death which, they imply, surround us.
The closeness of death is, as we have seen in 'Mayday on
Holderness', often paradoxically evident in a poem least explicitly
about war. The title of 'Relic' (*SP*, p. 53) carries a religious
resonance which, perhaps, suggests a celebration of that universal
fact of death, based on the bone-litter of a beach. Yet, even if that is
so, we are chilled by the opposing implications of the 'cold' deeps,
the 'darkness' in which 'cameraderie does not hold'; where
'Nothing touches but, clutching, devours' (p. 53). 'Cameraderie'
implies wartime friendships: intimate, but short-lived in the
universal torrent of self-destruction. The instinctual depths
sounded in poems like 'Relic' and 'To Paint A Water Lily' have
often a vitality, the vitality of a dance of death. Yet, as with the
'animal' poems, a human perspective is present, too — in 'Relic',
most notably in the last word: 'This curved jawbone did not
laugh/But gripped, gripped and is now a cenotaph'. That so small
and apparently insignificant an object can seem to take on such
immense proportions is a tribute to the poet's imagination, an
imagination here rooted in the memory of war, a war we are
obliged by annual ceremonies at the Cenotaph not to forget, but
which in Hughes is a reminder of the darker, hidden memory of the
instinctual drives which are so cruelly apparent in the midst of
battle.

　　Battle, especially the battle of bayonet charges and trench

fighting established by the First World War, concentrates attention upon what is immediately threatening, physical extinction, and brings into play the primary, instinctual responses. Hence the conjunction of war, the memory of war, and age-old, 'prehistoric' or pre-rational feelings in Hughes' poetry. A further development of this is evident in 'Ghost Crabs' (pp. 67–8), which is in a much freer, longer and more discursive form than the poems we have been considering so far in this chapter. In it, blind, fearsome, yet oddly grotesque and even comic forces are imagined lumbering in a 'slow mineral fury' through us as we lie asleep, barely ruffled by the dim consciousness of what is happening within and around us. 'Helmet crabs' are very primitive creatures of the spider family, and it is a characteristic Hughesian mix of natural observation, the memory of war, and an eruption of primitive forces, which produces those 'glistening nacelles' (another military metaphor) from the tide, 'Giant crabs, under flat skulls, staring inland/Like a packed trench of helmets' (p. 67).

The implications of 'Ghost Crabs' are, to say the least, disturbing. It seems as if there are forces working in and through us for which we cannot be responsible, since they are so basic to our natural selves — they are genetic, rather than divine, or historical. The 'ghost crabs' represent 'the turmoil of history, the convulsion/ In the roots of blood, in the cycles of concurrence' (p. 68). They are beneath everything, beyond order or conscious control — whether exercised by God or ourselves. As Hughes moves away from traditional beliefs, he moves away from traditional means of expression, too, towards a more enigmatic, symbolic and modernist realm, as we will see in the *Crow* sequence.

We can easily misunderstand, or misrepresent this fundamental aspect of Hughes's vision, his 'violence'. Perhaps the poem which has created the most misunderstanding, or which has been most misrepresented, but which is also widely recognised as one of his finest, is 'Hawk Roosting', from *Lupercal* (p. 43). It is a poem which above all established Hughes's early reputation — and notoriety, in some circles. The way it has been read, or misread, depending on your point of view, has determined the way much of his later work has been read — or misread. What do you think of it? Is it in any sense about war? Unlike 'To Paint a Water Lily', 'Hawk Roosting' has a strong narratorial presence: how does this affect your reading of the poem? At the same time, try comparing it with some of those we have already discussed, such as 'Six Young Men', or even earlier, 'The Hawk in the Rain' and 'The Jaguar', all of which may be said to deal in 'violence', but in different ways.

Hawk Roosting

I sit in the top of the wood, my eyes closed.
Inaction, no falsifying dream
Between my hooked head and hooked feet
Or in sleep rehearse perfect kills and eat.

The convenience of the high trees!
The air's buoyancy and the sun's ray
Are of advantage to me;
And the earth's face upward for my inspection.

My feet are locked upon the rough bark.
It took the whole of Creation
To produce my foot, my each feather:
Now I hold Creation in my foot

Or fly up, and revolve it all slowly —
I kill where I please because it is all mine.
There is no sophistry in my body:
My manners are tearing off heads —

The allotment of death.
For the one path of my flight is direct
Through the bones of the living.
No arguments assert my right:

The sun is behind me.
Nothing has changed since I began.
My eye has permitted no change.
I am going to keep things like this.

DISCUSSION

My first impression is one of *controlled* violence, expressed with
remarkable economy and brevity, and without any of Hughes's
occasional sledgehammer rhetoric. It is an austere poem, about
killing, rather than being killed. A monologue, it is told from the
point of view of a hawk sitting in the top of a wood, which gives it a
singular consistency and force, doesn't it? Unlike 'The Hawk in the
Rain', no distinction is drawn between the observing, human
intelligence and the creature observed. But what is it about?

The hawk is apparently in a solipsistic trance, self-admiring and
single-minded in pursuit of its end, which is the 'allotment of death'.

He says there is 'no sophistry in my body', 'No arguments' to 'assert my right'. This develops and emphasizes the opening idea that 'no falsifying dream' comes between the hawk's hooked head and hooked feet, reminding us, by contrast, of ourselves, limited as we are by the 'dream' of consciousness, which separates us from the beasts. Unlike the sense of dream in 'The Jaguar' or 'Out', here 'dream' suggests thought, ratiocination, the process that as it were interferes with, and distorts, the connection between impulse and action. In the words of Brutus, contemplating the death of Caesar: 'Between the acting of a dreadful thing/ And the first motion, all the interim is/Like a phantasma, or a hideous dream' (*Julius Caesar*, II, i, lines 63–5). But that dream is *conscience*: to put it aside is to try to become like an animal, a killing machine, without guilt or shame, for human consciousness also involves a moral sense.

Thus the hawk's natural function defines its nature; and the poem apparently reveals it glorying in what it is. The crucial question is: are we, too, invited to glory in what it is? Critics have taken this as the essential meaning of the poem, extending it to include a glorification of totalitarianism.[6] Yet the poem carefully avoids specifying any overtly social or historical aspect of its subject — 'The sun is behind me' may hint at a fighter plane zeroing in on its target, the 'flight' through 'the bones of the living' may remind us vividly of the horrible effect of gunfire, yet how far do such details invite identification with the poem's central consciousness? And is our identification *uncritical*? In the end, you have to decide for yourself whether the poem can be understood to glorify fascist militarism, or to what extent the charge against it is justified. But, as you will guess from what I have already said about the complexity of the whole issue of violence in Hughes's work, I do not myself take this view, which I consider a simplistic misreading.

There *are* poems by Hughes, especially some of the weaker 'war' poems (the weaker ones tend to get used to support the view that Hughes celebrates mindless violence), which imply a rather crude worship of big-chested brutality: for instance, 'The Ancient Heroes and the Bomber Pilot' (excluded from *Selected Poems*), in which the central figures are admiringly compared with his own puniness by a poet who imagines

> Their chariot-wheels tumbling the necks of screams,

> In a glory of hair and beard,
> They thinned down their fat fulsome blood in war,
> Replenishing both bed and board ...

This is far from the best Hughes, any more than 'The Retired Colonel' (*SP* p. 50) 'Who lived at the top end of our street', shot through with whisky and 'ancient courage', 'man-eating British lion/By a pimply age brought down'. Even more alarming, although equally unimpressive as a poem, is 'A Motorbike' (p. 213). Here the post-war peace is said to make all the young men of his village prisoners, the 'morning bus as bad as any labour truck,' and the 'foreman, the boss, as bad as the S.S.' Straying outside the metaphoric memory of war, into explicit socio-historical detail, betrays the worst of Hughes. But in 'Hawk Roosting', it seems to me, what we have is essentially a development of the view suggested in 'The Hawk in the Rain': namely, that the bird is subject to a delusion, a delusion which is attractive (and we are made to feel that), a delusion by which we may wish to live, but a delusion nonetheless.

If you are puzzled, you might like to look at the poem again, in particular, at the last line. What impact does it have on your impression of the poem as a whole? To me, the effect is similar to the double-take experienced at the end of 'The Thought-Fox': a moment of dramatic revelation, especially if read aloud.

'I am going to keep things like this': the line can only be read ironically, I feel. By this stage, there is something ludicrous about the huge pretensions of the hawk, its belief not only that the high trees, the air's buoyancy, the sun, the earth, are there for its convenience, but also, with sublime egoism, that the whole purpose of Creation was to produce its foot, each individual feather. Moreover, reading the surprisingly short sentences which make up the poem — the syntax of manic certitude — until, in the last stanza, we have four lines each made up of a complete sentence, confirms the realization of what the poem ultimately presents: a vision of the complete insanity of power.

The hawk thinks it has the power of God: it can hold that whole Creation which went into its making. In *Crow*, God is shown to labour under the same delusion. Here, there are social, historical implications, confirmed by Hughes's remark elsewhere that the hawk sounds 'like Hitler's familiar spirit'.[7] If the social or historical dimension seems to be omitted from Hughes' work, this is not necessarily because the poet is unaware of it; rather, in a poem such as 'Hawk Roosting', he goes straight to what seem to him to be the deeper undercurrents, and he does so in such a way that we are brought to share the delusion without the detachment possible where everything is spelled out in more overt detail. As Michael Hamburger has written, in the line 'My manners are tearing off heads —', the single word 'manners' is enough to make the connection between the ferocious ways of this predator and the ways of mankind.[8] Hughes's acknowledged, unremitting interest in violence serves a vision which is constantly aware of the massive ebb and flow of natural forces underlying all life and which is — as his treatment of the memory of war suggests — much more than a simple celebration of death or destruction. We would not want to attend to his poetry for very long if it were no more than that.

5. Hughes and Tradition

For all the unique power with which he does so, Hughes is not alone in registering the threatening memory of war in apparently innocent nature poems. Consider the following, by Edmund Blunden (1896–1974):

The Midnight Skaters

The hop-poles stand in cones,
    The icy pond lurks under,
The pole-tops steeple to the thrones
    Of stars, sound gulfs of wonder;
But not the tallest there, 'tis said,
Could fathom to the pond's black bed.

Then is not death at watch
    Within those secret waters?
What wants he but to catch
    Earth's heedless sons and daughters?
With but a crystal parapet
Between, he has his engines set.

Then on, blood shouts, on, on,
    Twirl, wheel and whip above him,
Dance on this ball-floor thin and wan,
    Use him as though you love him;
Court him, elude him, reel and pass,
And let him hate you through the glass.

(1925)

What do you make of it? A strangely menacing quality emerges, doesn't it, within the quietly pastoral setting? Blunden is not usually admitted to be a precursor of Hughes: he is usually shunted off into the literary-historical category of 'Georgian', by which is meant 'safe', if not 'boring', the characteristically quiescent, domestic note of the popular poetry of the early decades of this century. But, as in 'To Paint A Water Lily', or 'Pike', the suggestion of malevolent, battling forces waiting and watching from below is unignorable, as is the striking fact that they are imagined in terms reminiscent of the War — in stanza 2 death is 'at watch' with 'engines set' beyond a 'crystal parapet'. The confluence of 'nature' and 'war' in Hughes's poetry may be less surprising, less original, than it seems at first glance.

But this is surely because, in the poems which reach us most effectively, he touches on the dimly familiar forces at work within ourselves and our culture — forces he could not be alone in recognising. Another way of putting this would be to say that Hughes is, in an important sense, a poet working within a broad tradition, the recent English tradition. But what, exactly, does 'tradition' mean here? And how do we find it out?

In studying poetry, rather than simply reading it for our own pleasure, we are often encouraged to think about 'sources' and 'influences'. The underlying assumption is that by comparing a particular poet's work with that of others, especially predecessors, we will be able to discover and define that poet's individual essence. But, as we have seen, uncovering what is individual in a poet's work, even in the limited sense of the personal, is not straightforward. Nor is trying to find a poet's relationship with other poets and writers, or 'tradition'. Yet such considerations can be both helpful and interesting; and, with other aspects of the study of a poet, should eventually bring us back to the poems with increased understanding and pleasure. In this chapter, I will compare some of Hughes's poems with a handful by other poets, mainly those with whom he has most frequently been compared, on the grounds either that he has been influenced by, or resembles them. In this way, we should get an idea of how far he relates to what might be defined as a tradtion in English poetry; and how far he is moving away from that tradition. To the school audiences addressed by *Poetry in the Making*, Hughes observed that

> The work of most good poets is written out of some especially affecting and individual experience which they have undergone at some time, or perhaps which, because of something in their nature, keeps happening to them again and again. The wider this experience is, the more of ordinary life it includes, the greater the poet, as a rule. But some very great poets have written out of quite a limited and peculiar experience. Wordsworth's greatest poetry seems to be rooted in two or three rather similar experiences he had as a boy among the Cumberland mountains.[1]

This seems to put the emphasis where it should be: on the poet's experience. Experience is, after all, the most important source and influence, isn't it? But, especially in the case of poets and writers, that experience is not necessarily direct — hence the impact upon Hughes of his father's memories of war — and it usually includes the experience of reading. We forget too often that reading, especially for writers, *is* an experience. You can see what I mean from Hughes's own words: not for the first or only time in his remarks about poetry of poets, he refers to one of the great Romantics, Wordsworth. As I suggested earlier, Hughes's work can fruitfully be related to that of Wordsworth — and his fellow-Romantics, Coleridge and Blake. His whole conception of poetry, and the poet's role, seems fundamentally akin to theirs, however contemporary the subject and manner of his work may be.

This is more than a matter of verbal echoes or allusions — although these can easily be found. For instance, the 'midnight moment's forest' of 'The Thought-Fox', is reminiscent of Blake's 'Tyger! Tyger! burning bright/In the forests of the night' ('The Tyger'). Indeed, if you compare the whole of 'The Thought-Fox' with Blake's poem, you will find, I think, that it is an *idea* or *experience* that they share: of a symbolic creature which disturbs us with its mysterious challenge to the imagination. Consider the following extract from Wordsworth's *The Prelude*, the massive autobiographical poem which occupied him for some forty years. Do you see any similarity with Hughes's poetry?

> Ye Presences of Nature in the Sky
> And on the earth! Ye Visions of the hills!
> And Souls of lonely places! can I think
> A vulgar hope was yours when ye employed
> Such ministry, when ye through many a year

> Haunting me thus among my boyish sports,
> On caves and trees, upon the woods and hills,
> Impressed upon all forms the characters
> Of danger or desire; and thus did make
> The surface of the universal earth
> With triumph and delight, with hope and fear,
> Work like a sea?
>
> (*The Prelude*, 1850 edn., Book I, lines 464–475)

DISCUSSION

Isn't there a clear similarity in the way each poet conceives the influence of nature, and humanity's relationship with nature? As Hughes points out, Wordsworth's greatest poetry is rooted in his experiences as a boy in the Cumberland mountains. There he became aware of, as he puts it, the 'presences' of nature, which haunted his 'boyish sports', making the 'surface of the universal earth' informed with human emotions, with 'triumph and delight, with hope and fear'. Similarly, much of Hughes's work, ostensibly about nature, is on closer inspection found to be about those feelings which nature has inspired in him. Like Wordsworth, Hughes's central concern is with nature but it is nature imagined in terms of an intense, individual responsiveness which, it is hoped, may quicken the awareness of the whole community. The visionary, quasi-religious overtones to Wordsworth's poetic enterprise are comparable to what we can often sense in Hughes, who believes that 'the spirit that worked through Wordsworth and Coleridge and Blake chose them for its parables'.[2]

But if Hughes can be associated with the Romantics in this way, it was their more recent successors who seemed to his earliest critics to lie behind his work. When *The Hawk in the Rain* first appeared, the surprising new voice noticed by Edwin Muir was met with the accusation 'derivative'. Derivative of whom? G. M. Hopkins, W. B. Yeats, Dylan Thomas and D. H. Lawrence were the most frequently cited names, as poets whose work had obviously influenced Hughes — themselves, as it happens, clear inheritors of the Romantic tradition. How just was the charge? Take Hopkins, in particular, one of his best-known poems, 'The Windhover'. Read it through carefully, and then reread the title-poem 'The Hawk in the Rain', printed above, p. 1. Are these poems similar, or are there overriding differences? (Note: 'sillion' means furrow.)

The Windhover:
To Christ our Lord

I caught this morning morning's minion, kingdom
  of daylight's dauphin, dapple-dawn-dawn Falcon, in his riding
  Of the rolling level underneath him steady air, and striding
High there, how he rung upon the rein of a wimpling wing
In his ecstasy! then off, off forth on swing,
  As a skate's heel sweeps smooth on a bow-bend: the hurl and
gliding
  Rebuffed the big wind. My heart in hiding
Stirred for a bird, — the achieve of, the mastery of the thing!

Brute beauty and valour and act, oh, air, pride, plume, here
  Buckle! AND the fire that breaks from thee then, a billion
Times told lovelier, more dangerous, O my chevalier!

  No wonder of it: shéer plód makes plough down sillion
Shine, and blue-bleak embers, ah my dear,
  Fall, gall themselves, and gash gold-vermilion.

DISCUSSION

Again, the very opening line of the Hopkins poem seems familiar,
doesn't it? 'I imagine this midnight moment's forest ...' 'The
Thought-Fox' echoes 'I caught this morning morning's minion' in
sound and structure, if not in meaning. But it is the comparison
with 'The Hawk in the Rain' which yields more interesting
associations. This poem seems to owe a lot in both conception and
manner to Hopkins. Like 'The Windhover', 'The Hawk in the Rain'
offers a breathtaking enactment of the power and energy of a bird.
Hughes's emphatic rhythms and strongly marked stresses are very
similar to Hopkins's, as are the violent verbs, extended adjective
phrases and run-on lines — all used to evoke an almost physical
sensation of striving and ecstasy, the state of being identified in
Hughes's poem, with the hawk, and with the kestrel in Hopkins's.
This does make 'The Hawk in the Rain' so similar to 'The
Windhover' as to seem derivative.

  But, as you may well have begun to protest, there *are* differences
too, aren't there? And strong, if not overriding, differences as well.
As Hopkins's sub-title suggests, and his poem confirms, he
identifies the bird's state of being with Christ: grace of movement

becomes divine grace. Hughes's poem is also religious in feeling, but not specifically Christian: he evokes awe for the possibility of perfect power and mastery in nature which can transcend itself (the bird meeting the weather coming to smash him 'maybe in his own time') to the point of defeating death. Both poems, I think, exploit a dualism between matter and spirit: matter as the earth, where mortality, or death resides; spirit as the height of the sky which seems to hold out hope of escape into timelessness. The narrator of 'The Windhover' imagines himself as a 'heart' in 'hiding', down where 'shéer plód makes plough down sillion/Shine'; but stirred by the high striding above him of the 'Falcon, in his riding/Of the rolling underneath him steady air'. Hughes's narrator is clutched by the clay of the earth like a 'dogged grave'; but he too is aware of the presence above him, the hawk who (and the word 'hawk' is suspended at the end of the line to mimic this) 'Effortlesly at height hangs his still eye'.

But for Hughes, the sky is closed, the horizon is a trap; and death brings no redemptive possibility; whereas for Hopkins, the fall of the bird to earth is conceived as a kind of splendid triumph, — invoking the Christian paradox of the fall of man in a way never attempted by Hughes, who is more likely (in 'A Childish Prank' for example) to parody the fall. Hopkins's 'gash gold-vermilion' reveals the bright new colours of hope: for him, resurrection is a real possibility. Hughes's hawk deludes itself when it seems to meet death in its own time. Hughes is, like Hopkins, something of a visionary: but their visions are fundamentally different. 'The Hawk in the Rain' suggests an unflinching stoicism; 'The Windhover', faith in an afterlife. Hopkins has the confidence of his concluding consolation — a confidence confirmed, perhaps, by his use of the more traditional, strict form: 'The Windhover' is a sonnet, whereas Hughes's poem is written in his typically unrhymed, looser stanza-pattern.

You could well also compare 'The Hawk in the Rain' with Dylan Thomas's, 'Over Sir John's Hill', with which it also has close similarities of manner and theme. But the point has been made, I think: that closeness on this level does not preclude basic differences, differences which are surely more interesting in the end than the similarities which may be identified? If so, this is because, for all his 'derivativeness', Hughes is struggling with his own vision.

Let us try another example. As I've mentioned, D. H. Lawrence is also a poet whose work is often referred to in discussions of Hughes. It is not difficult to see why in a general way, but, again, it is fruitful to pursue a specific poem.

Hughes included the following Lawrence poem in *Poetry in the Making* as an example of the concentrated focus upon a subject which poets need to learn. Read it now, working out for yourself what you think it is about, exactly, and how Lawrence gets his effects. Then read 'Gnat-Psalm' (*SP*, pp. 110–12) which, as the title suggests, also takes a tiny insignificant creature as its central focus. And ask yourself: what do the two poems have in common? Are they essentially about the same thing, or not? Where do they differ? (Note: 'Winged Victory', i.e., 'The Winged Victory of Samothrace', larger-than-life Classical statue in the Louvre)

Mosquito

When did you start your tricks,
Monsieur?

What do you stand on such high legs for?
Why this length of shredded shank,
You exaltation?

Is it so that you shall lift your centre of gravity upwards
And weigh no more than air as you alight upon me,
Stand upon me weightless, you phantom?

I heard a woman call you the Winged Victory
In sluggish Venice.
You turn your head towards your tail and smile.

How can you put so much devilry
Into that translucent phantom shred
Of a frail corpus?

Queer, with your thin wings and your streaming legs,
How you sail like a heron, or a dull clot of air,
A nothingness.

Yet what an aura surrounds you;
Your evil little aura, prowling, and casting numbness on my mind.
That is your trick, your bit of filthy magic:
Invisibility, and the anaesthetic power
To deaden my attention in your direction.

But I know your game now, streaky sorcerer.
Queer, how you stalk and prowl the air
In circles and evasions, enveloping me,
Ghoul on wings
Winged Victory.

Settle, and stand on long thin shanks
Eyeing me sideways, and cunningly conscious that I am aware,
You speck.

I hate the way you lurch off sideways into the air
Having read my thoughts against you.

Come then, let us play at unawares,
And see who wins in this sly game of bluff.
Man or mosquito.

You don't know that I exist, and I don't know that you exist.
Now then!

It is your trump,
It is your hateful little trump,
You pointed fiend,
Which shakes my sudden blood to hatred of you:
It is your small, high, hateful bugle in my ear.

Why do you do it?
Surely it is bad policy.
They say you can't help it.

If that is so, then I believe a little in Providence protecting the
    innocent.
But it sounds so amazingly like a slogan,
A yell of triumph as you snatch my scalp.

Blood, red blood
Super-magical
Forbidden liquor.

I behold you stand
For a second enspasmed in oblivion,
Obcenely ecstasied
Sucking live blood,
My blood.

Such silence, such suspended transport,
Such gorging,
Such obscenity of trespass.

You stagger
As well as you may.
Only your accursed hairy frailty,

Your own imponderable weightlessness
Saves you, wafts you away on the very draught my anger makes
in its snatching.

Away with a paean of derision,
You winged blood-drop.

Can I not overtake you?
Are you one too many for me,
Winged Victory?
Am I not mosquito enough to out-mosquito you?

Queer what a big stain my sucked blood makes
Beside the infinitesimal faint smear of you!
Queer, what a dim dark smudge you have disappeared into!

DISCUSSION

Let us take the Lawrence poem first. About a mosquito? Yes; but
even more about the narrator's responses to it. The presence of this
tiny, apparently insignificant creature is evoked with marvellous
accuracy: its tricky 'circles and evasions', the way it seems always
to 'lurch off sideways into the air' when you try and catch it, that
'hateful little trump', the 'bugle' in your ear when you realize
you've lost the battle and been stung, your blood then obscenely
gorging it. Its potential strangeness is also caught, the 'queerness' as
it is called, of so much 'devilry' and 'exaltation' in such a tiny,
'weightless' phantom, a 'nothingness'. In a way absurd, calling the
creature Winged Victory heightens the exaggeration, but equally
the humour, of the whole conception. Perhaps even more
unexpected than the choice of subject, is the extraordinary way the
lines of the poem are composed, varying so much in length and
stanza-pattern, and yet clearly helping the quick, colloquial feel of
it all. Lawrence was often attacked for his apparent lack of formal
organisation, but defended himself well when he said of his poetry
that is was 'the unrestful, ungraspable poetry of the sheer present,
poetry whose very permanency lies in its wind-like transit.'[3] What
he offers here is an intuition of the vital energy of nature: an
intuition prompted by the barely noticeable, non-human creatures
whose mystery we cannot or will not bother to explore. The
hyperbolic wit of 'Mosquito' should not obscure the underlying
apprehension of another world than ours, which surrounds as it
penetrates our everyday ordinary lives.

Hughes usually chooses more obviously impressive predators upon which to meditate: a jaguar, hawk, pike or fox (although there is also 'The Rat's Dance', a kind of companion-piece to this poem, *SP*, p. 100). But with 'Gnat-Psalm' he has, like Lawrence, exploited the barely noticeable attributes of a familiar little creature for similarly large purposes, has he not? Perhaps though, as the title suggests, stressing the visionary, quasi-religious potential of his reflections much more than 'Mosquito'? The overtones of 'psalm' are developed throughout the poem: from the opening metaphoric link between the wild hieroglyphics, the faint, obscure singing, of gnats, and the sacred songs of the Old Testament, towards establishing a similarly exuberant, hyperbolic vision. The gnats, like the mosquito, may be tiny, nearly nothing at all; but, viewed apart from the usual, dismissive human attitude towards such creatures, they can become 'angels', even 'God'. Again, like Lawrence, Hughes exploits an (for him, this was in *Wodwo*) unconventional, unpatterned verse form to represent the movement of the gnats and the poem's reflections upon them:

Dancing

Dancing

In the glove shadows of the sycamore

A dance never to be altered

A dance giving their bodies to be burned

Their meaning, short-lived and ephemeral as they are, is large: they are bits of primal energy, a mere glimpse of which 'Rolls my staring skull slowly away into outer space' as if knocked outside the familiar, bodily world by this sudden, surprising revelation.

So far I have been stressing what Hughes and Lawrence have in common here, although there is a lot more to be said about both poems. But it is important to realise how close an affinity there is between the two poets, which is much more that a mere coincidence of interest in the vitality of nature. As you can see from 'Mosquito' and 'Gnat-Psalm', there is in both an alert fineness of observation, a responsiveness to the creaturely world, which is truly remarkable; but there is also a profound interest in showing, through a confrontation between the human and non-human worlds, a strange and exciting mystery at the heart of things – a mystery which encourages a sense of awe bordering on the religious, but without finally offering any specifically religious message. The element of *confrontation* involved is essential, and part of what leads us to distinguish both poets from the earlier Romantic tradition, especially Wordsworth, in whose work there is a more passive, moralizing approach to nature. Hughes and Lawrence dramatise encounters between human and animal which ultimately subvert that tradition, a tradition in which the human subject is always at the centre — by obliging us to imagine ourselves merely another part of the heaving universe of matter. Hence the possibility of a mosquito or a gnat signifying more than the human being who notices or imagines them.

Of course, there is a paradox here, isn't there? In that the whole enterprise is itself the product of human consciousness and imagination; but the point is that we are to follow these intuitions in to the world outside ourselves, beyond our familiar grasp. Both poets seem to write out of an awareness of such paradoxes, too: this helps explain the common thread of wit and humour, unexpected, exaggerated, and delightful. The gnats' 'frail eyes and crepuscular temperaments' are as superbly ridiculous as the mosquito's Gallic 'tricks' with his rapier-sting, like a fencing-master dancing about on 'high legs'.

Yet 'Mosquito' is more consistently funny than the Hughes poem, isn't it? Or at least, it is light-hearted; whereas 'Gnat-Psalm' takes us into realms of horror unimagined by Lawrence. I am thinking of more than the obvious Christian references, to nails and suffering, in stanza six of 'Gnat-Psalm', but also of the allusions in the stanza beginning 'Their little bearded faces', allusions unavailable to Lawrence. By drawing on the Old Testament, the poem alerts us to the terrible climax in our time of the long history of persecution endured by the Jews. Lawrence breaks with the notion of nature as comforting, consoling and morally uplifting; a notion embodied in most English poetry of his time, 'Georgian' poetry (Blunden's 'Midnight Skaters' was exceptional). Hughes takes this further, to find in nature an image of the awful cruelty of our own species. His fascination with this side of things leads to a different kind of poetry in the end, despite the affinity with Lawrence apparent from 'Mosquito' and 'Gnat-Psalm'. Lawrence prefers, it seems, to close off his poem rather too neatly after the wonderful looseness of its progress, by means of the exclamatory 'Queer, what a dim dark smudge' the mosquito has become; with Hughes, we are left with a strange and horrifying image which does not let us off the hook quite so quickly or easily. I do not mean to be unfair to Lawrence. As has been pointed out[4] there are other ways in which his poetry may be seen to be more rather than less effective than Hughes's — for instance, in the extent to which, unlike Hughes, he appears not to claim to possess the being of his chosen creatures: 'I didn't know his God', remarks the narrator of 'Fish', whereas Hughes imagines he does.

It seems right then, to invoke Lawrence when looking at Hughes; but we do need to consider what we mean, in relation to specific examples of their work, before we can arrive at justifiable generalisations about the connections between them. What we can now say, is that Hughes is clearly a deeply English poet, his work steeped in the Romantic and post-Romantic traditions of English poetry; but he has also — as we would expect of a poet with his power to surprise us — gone his own way. Lawrence provides an apt comparison, since he, too, went his own way. Indeed, in a direction which highlights the path chosen by Hughes, away from the passively moralising tradition dominant since Wordsworth and (for all Wordsworth's continuing influence), towards a more radical, darkly amoral yet witty strain. This is what we find as we move from Hughes's earlier, apparently milder and more controlled poems (in *The Hawk in the Rain* and *Lupercal*) towards the *Crow* and *Cave Birds* (1978) cycles. *Wodwo*, as I have already suggested, may be understood as a turning-point. What is new and surprising about the *Crow* poems and their immediate successors is not only the shock generated by their black humour, by the relentless, extravagant nihilism of poem after poem; but also the striking departure from work which seems, for all its initial impact, to operate within familiar traditions. In, for example, 'A Childish Prank' (which we looked at on p. 7), there is a newly intense, spare and surreal voice, typically *modern* in its uncompromising toughness, and its freedom from established poetic norms.

This characteristically modern quality in Hughes's work has led to comparisons with a number of modern poets — significantly, poets not operating within the English traditions: the Americans Wallace Stevens, William Carlos Williams and, of course, Sylvia Plath, who introduced her husband to American poetry; and the Eastern European poets Vasko Popa, Miroslav Holub and János Pilinszky, in whom Hughes has taken much interest. It has been argued that there is a clear similarity between Hughes's aesthetic and that of Wallace Stevens, a similiarity of 'preoccupations' and 'some key-images' in the *Crow* cycle, expressive of 'an unmoralized play of imagination.'[5] This is helpful, and you might want to pursue, for example, a comparison between Stevens's 'Thirteen Ways of Looking at a Blackbird' (which Hughes included in his

Poetry in the Making), and 'Crow's Last Stand' (*SP*, p. 127), considering just how their common playful and fantastic vision of nature seems to operate.

But in my view a stronger and more interesting connection may be established by looking at any of the Eastern European poets Hughes has helped to promote. Stevens's dry, mandarin wit belongs to a pre-war world:

> I do not know which to prefer,
> The beauty of inflexions
> Or the beauty of innuendos,
> The blackbird whistling
> Or just after.

('Thirteen Ways of Looking at a Blackbird')

Hughes's crow belongs to an altogether wilder, more broadly humorous and yet darker realm, riddled with an awareness of the European memory of mass destruction:

> Burning
>
>   burning
>
>   burning

('Crow's Last Stand')

Hughes has chosen to face the terrible reality of evil with which we all, nowadays, think we are familiar, but of which he wishes to remind us. And he has been drawn to those poets who seem to him 'closer to the common reality, in which we have to live if we are to survive', as he put it in his Introduction to a selection of Popa's poetry.[6] Here is a poem from that selection. Please read it now, and ask yourself what, if anything, it seems to be about; and what *kind* of poetry it seems to be. You may find that your answer to the second question helps you to work out an answer to the first.

The dream of the quartz pebble

A hand appeared out of the earth
Flung the pebble into the air

Where is the pebble
It hasn't come back to earth
It hasn't climbed up to heaven

What's become of the pebble
Have the heights devoured it
Has it turned into a bird

Here is the pebble
Stubborn it has stayed in itself
Not in heaven nor in earth

It obeys itself
Amongst the worlds a world

DISCUSSION

How can a pebble dream? The title itself suggests that we are far
from the familiar world; and yet, isn't a pebble one of the most
familiar things in our world? And despite the poem's attempt to
make that most ordinary of everyday material objects turn into
something else, 'Stubborn it has stayed in itself'. Although the poem
seems to leave our own logical, fact-ridden universe, there is a clear
logic within it, which seems to end up insisting that — well, a
pebble is a pebble, and that is enough. We have entered the world
of allegory, or myth. There is no human being here, only a hand,
magically appearing to throw the pebble up. If you have ever come
across a surrealist painting, by Joan Miró or Salvador Dali, for
example, you would not, perhaps, have been too surprised by this:
there, too, you find fragments of the body, things apparently
arbitrarily produced, a dream-like, irrational world, vivid, shocking
and/or amusing. Or if you know T. S. Eliot's famous lines

> Let us go then, you and I,
> When the evening is spread out against the sky
> Like a patient etherised upon a table ...
> ('The Love Song of J. Alfred Prufrock')

you may recognise the kind of outrageous metaphoric comparison
beloved of the surrealists, yoking together the most unlikely things,
in a deadpan, often playful way. But to what purpose or effect? To
suggest, perhaps, the irrelevance of the old forms and subject
matter for our modern world, from which the human seems almost
excluded? To suggest the one remaining power, of the imagination,
that might order things, and offer a little understanding? To create
new myths? There are, I am suggesting, many possibilities for this
kind of enigmatic, parabolic poetry. Certainly it is typically modern
in its pared-down, suggestive, 'mythical' obscurity: and this is also

Joan Miró: Person Throwing a Stone at a Bird. 1926. Oil on canvas, 29 × 36¼" (73.7 × 92.1 cm). Collection the Museum of Modern Art, New York. Purchase.

true of some of Hughes's most powerful poems. One final example, which you can compare with the Popa: try reading 'How Water Began To Play' (p. 133), one of the *Crow* poems without the crow. What does it have in common with 'The dream of the quartz pebble'? What does it mean?

DISCUSSION

Like Popa's little poem, this carries with it an air of dealing in basics, having its own logic, and of being at a somewhat obscure angle to the familiar world. It has to do with water, water wanting to live, trying various means of doing so, and then, finally, lying 'Utterly worn out', but also 'utterly clear'. Repetition and balance seem to be the main organising features, as with the Popa poem. Like a nursery rhyme, or riddle, or some combination of these; like a 'primitive' song, or myth, the oral poetry of non or pre-literate cultures. To know that it was originally published as one of 'Two Eskimo Songs' should, then, come as no surprise.

In leaving behind the familiar, post-Romantic poetic traditions in this way, Hughes is, then, not alone: he is doing what other modern writers have done, or are doing, as the comparison with Popa makes clear. It is a characteristically modern project to try and return to the 'primitive', to deploy ancient, folkloric skills and traditions in an attempt to recreate a mythical order in the midst of our disorder. So even when he might seem most unique, most unfamiliar, Hughes can still be connected with identifiable tradition. This is because, as T. S. Eliot remarked many years ago now, 'No poet, no artist of any art, has his complete meaning alone … You cannot value him alone; you must set him, for contrast and comparison, among the dead.'[7] Well – and among the living too! That is what 'tradition' means.

6. The Satire of Survival

Most English poets, according to Ted Hughes, spend their apprentice years 'bowing and scraping' to their predecessors. 'It is part of our patrician and conservative culture', he believes, that 'we should be almost paralysed by the examples of our seniors ... Our beginners in poetry, like our lower ranks in war, seem to have lacked initiative somewhat, in this century.'[1] Hughes himself could hardly be accused of lacking initiative, so perhaps he has earned the right to accuse others. For all his deep immersion in the stream of native English verse from its Anglo-Saxon origins to the present, he has always gone his own way, dipping into whatever serves his purpose, from Eskimo legend to Greek myth, from Celtic cosmology to the Bible. This is a function of how he sees the role of a poet today.

Hughes's radical eclecticism has, on occasion, led to results either foolish or absurd, although it has also ensured a seriousness of import to which we should attend. Both aspects are most evident in his works from *Wodwo* to *Moortown*; that is, products of the late sixties and seventies, when the poet's own personal response to the deaths of Sylvia Plath and Assia Gutsmann seems to have coincided with the sudden growth of interest in alternative modes of thought, expression and action which marked the contemporary cultural scene. Hughes became involved in such experimental projects as the mystical, Promethean drama *Orghast*, for which he invented a form of rhythmical discourse derived from Anglo-Saxon, Norse, Greek, Latin and Avesta (the ceremonial language of Zoroastrianism). The play survives as fragments in an account of the collaboration with Peter Brooks's International Centre for Theatre Research in Persepolis, Iran, for which it was created in 1971.[2] *Gaudete* (1972) was another attempt to explore new ways of expressing a deep-rooted, despairing quest for meaning and hope which began as a rough film scenario in 1964, and was recently (1986) dramatised. It is a bizarre poem which delves into myth, legend and religion as it relates the blood-soaked adventures of an Anglican clergyman abducted by spirits into 'the other world'. Less extended, but also relying upon archaic myths, were the fragmentary sequences *Prometheus on his Crag, Adam and the Sacred Nine* and *Earth-Numb*, all of which began some time before Hughes put them together with *Moortown Elegies* into *Moortown* (1979). None of these works have been more than fitfully successful; nor, in my view, have they deserved much success. How unlike the bird sequence *Crow*, which first began to appear in 1967, and which sold no less than 20,000 copies between its publication as a book in October 1970 and April 1974 — a quite remarkable feat for a volume of poems by a single author.[3] Continuing the successful idea of using a semi-mythical bird-like creature as the basis for a sequence, Hughes then also began a new collection in 1974, which became *Cave Birds* (1978). But *Crow* remains the major achievement of this period, and I have therefore chosen to focus upon it here. It is a persuasive instance of that unique potential to touch upon the deeper springs of fear and hope which, I suggested in my Introduction, characterises the best poetry of our own time. It has also been the cause of heated debate among poetry readers and critics.

What all these projects suggest is that, unlike most English poets of this century — except, perhaps, D. H. Lawrence — Hughes is a firmly modernist writer; in the sense that he sees his age as an age of crisis, of irreversible decay in the ethical-metaphysical system of enlightened, Western European culture; and he therefore attempts, in such extreme, experimental works, to express a personal vision defining what he considers minimally necessary for human survival. In a post-Christian age, or at least one in which the whole structure of beliefs associated with Christianity is disintegrating, other myths must be created, or rediscovered; and Hughes will ransack any culture for what he wants — a task made easier by his long familiarity with anthropology. Hughes attempts to go beyond earlier modernists such as T. S. Eliot or Ezra Pound, who also felt assailed by the breakdown of Western civilised values signalled by the First World War but who, nevertheless, felt it was possible to find 'fragments' to shore up against the 'ruins' (*The Waste Land*, 1921–2). Instead, he has become sharply aware that he operates at a time when the word 'incinerate' (which turns up again and again in *Crow*) has become horribly commonplace. Our collective memory — which, as our 'bard', he feels he cannot but help express

— now includes not only the shattered, body-strewn landscape of Gallipoli and the Somme, but also the oven-fires of Auschwitz and, looming over it all, Hiroshima.

In the *Crow* poem 'Notes for a Little Play', for example (*SP*, p. 130), Hughes imagines a world in which there are just 'Two survivors, moving in the flames blindly'; they are 'Mutations — at home in the nuclear glare.'[4] Such poetry anticipates the worst which may befall us, the thought of which alone, however much it tempts the imagination, finally defeats it. Which may help explain why so much of what Hughes produced during the sixties and seventies fails to convince, for all its profound ambitions. The problem is that such poetry may go so far from the everyday reality it aims to undermine, that it loses its audience.

How, then, to come to grips with it? We have already glanced at some of the *Crow* poems, but I would like now to try and confront the cycle as a whole — although still within the limitations of space available here, where we can do no more than look at a handful of the sixty-seven poems which appeared in the expanded 1972 edition. What we can do is try and consider three questions. What kind of poetry is this? What is it saying? And how far does the project as a whole seem to succeed?

'In our time', Hughes noted in 1962, 'the heroic sturggle is not to become a hero but to remain a living creature simply.'[5] This struggle was central to *Crow* from its inception, as we may gather from the fact the remark was made in an admiring introduction the poet wrote for an exhibition by the American artist-printer, Leonard Baskin, whose invitation to Hughes to write a series of poems to accompany some of his drawings and engravings (as you can tell from the drawing on p. 62, and the cover of *Selected Poems*) show bird-like creatures with disturbingly anthropomorphic features. Hughes's interest in them was evidently enormous, since, when the *Crow* cycle had ground to a halt and he saw more of the same, he was inspired to create the 'alchemical bird drama', *Cave Birds*, in which Baskin's drawings and his poems alternate, page by page. Several of the poems in *Cave Birds* are incomprehensible without their accompanying illustrations. The *Crow* poems are more free-standing.

First, read through all the *Crow* poems included in *Selected Poems* (pp. 115–34), to get a general sense of the sequence. Now, let us look at the very first words of *Crow: From the Life and Songs of the Crow* — to give the book its full title, since it was intended to become an epic folk tale in prose with the Crow songs interspersed (a project, like others, never completed, however). The following words are from the opening 'Two Legends' (not reprinted in

Cover drawing of Crow, by Leonard Baskin (Olwyn Hughes).

Selected Poems). Try reading the words aloud (or listen to Hughes reading them on record) and ask yourself: how does this feel? Is it like any of Hughes's earlier verse, say 'The Hawk in the Rain' or 'Pike' or 'Wodwo'? And what is it *about*? Does the heavily repetitive structure of it remind you of anything else, any other form of poetic incantation?

Two Legends

I

Black was the without eye
Black the within tongue
Black was the heart
Black the liver, black the lungs
Unable to suck in light
Black the blood in its loud tunnel
Black the bowels packed in furnace
Black too the muscles
Striving to pull out into the light
Black the nerves, black the brain
With its tombed visions
Black also the soul, the huge stammer
Of the cry that, swelling, could not
Pronounce its sun.

DISCUSSION

Like several of the earlier poems, this is poundingly alive, very physical — and, I would suggest, rather disturbing. What does it mean? Poems like 'The Thought-Fox', 'Pike' or even 'Wodwo', for all the latter's initial obscurity, were not too difficult to follow, were they? And, as we have seen, they approximate to the traditional forms of English verse, with 'Wodwo' moving perhaps the furthest away. This, on the other hand, is altogether something *other*, is it not?

And yet ... is it? 'Wodwo' wasn't about any real, identifiable beast, rather it evoked some mysterious, almost mythical presence, which the poet was apparently trying to catch unawares, to identify, as it snooped about in his imagination. And the language, the structure, the form of the poem expressed this. The *Crow* poems are also about some creature — a bird, but a bird less like the familiar scavenger you might find pecking at a bit of offal beside the road (although Hughes's Crow is that) than, again, like some mysterious, almost mythical presence. It is a presence which, the terms of its appearance imply, would reveal something serious and important to us, if we could only track it down. And the language, structure and form of the *Crow* poems express this, too. How can we tell? Not simply from these opening words, but they do give us a clue or two, as does the second of the 'Two Legends'. Both legends bear a suspicious resemblance to the familiar accounts of creation which appear in Genesis, a resemblance which, however, turns the Bible upside-down. The opening, intoning simple words and phrases over and over again, is like a religious incantation, isn't it? It is an incantation calling up a vision of total darkness which is nevertheless somehow alive with power, with energy, with *potential* for creation. Creation has not happened; but we can feel its pulse.

Thus, the muscles are 'striving to pull out into the light', and the soul stammers hugely as it tries to 'pronounce' the sun — that is, the source of all light. So light is also language, and language, the Word. Throughout the poems that follow, by means of this consciously primitive, stammering, struggling language, we hear and we witness an attempt of humankind's soul to create, that is, understand itself, by means of language. With the second 'legend', the crow comes in:

II

> Black is the wet otter's head, lifted.
> Black is the rock, plunging in foam.
> Black is the gall lying on the bed of the blood
>
> Black is the earth-globe, one inch under,
> An egg of blackness
> Where sun and moon alternate their weathers
>
> To hatch a crow, a black rainbow
> Bent in emptiness
>
>   over emptiness
>
> But flying

Out of the time when 'the earth was without form, and void, and darkness was upon the face of the deep' (Genesis, chapter 1, verse 2), God hatches, not day and night, not mankind, but — Crow, a 'black rainbow'. Instead of order coming out of the primeval chaos, instead of the hopeful, ultimately optimistic vision of the Old Testament, reflected in God's covenant with mankind, that rainbow which promised a relationship never again to be severed by flood and catastrophe (Genesis, chapter 9, verses 9–13), here is a 'black rainbow/Bent in emptiness/over emptiness'. This promise means nothing, except, perhaps, more catastrophes — as we shall see. But — and it's a big but — there *is* a crow, 'flying'. *Something* exists. What is it? An aspect of our nature, of our primal relationship to matter and to spirit, apparently. Like Blake's 'Tyger' or Yeats' swans, it's a mythical, symbolic creature, not limited to one poem, instead a creature we shall follow through many adventures, tests and ordeals, as it twists and turns to escape easy definition, and to evoke a multitude of responses. As I suggested earlier, with *Wodwo*, Hughes's treatment of the animal world, his ostensible major subject all along, became radically different. It became freed from almost all ties to the actual attributes of the animals evoked. And in *Crow* Hughes goes a step further: the real attributes of his creature take on a surreal, mythical dimension. Everyday reality has become even more suspect than it appeared in *Wodwo*. The conventions of language have become as questionable as the nature of the experience which language tries to shape and communicate. These poems appear in an original, bare and fragmentary dialect — yet one composed of the scraps of folklore, myth and religion which formerly provided us with an explanation of ourselves and our world, and so one riddled with associations from the past, as the Biblical echoes alone (there are other sources too) suggest.

Hughes has said that

> The first idea of *Crow* was really an idea of style. In folktales the prince going on the adventure comes to the stable full of beautiful horses and he needs a horse for the next stage and the king's daughter advises him to take none of the beautiful horses that he'll be offered but to choose the dirty, scabby little foal. You see, I throw out the eagles and choose the Crow. The idea was originally just to write his songs, the songs that a Crow would sing. In other words, songs with no music whatsoever, in a super-simple and super-ugly language which would in a way shed everything except just what he wanted to say without any other consideration and that's the basis of the style of the whole thing. I get near it in a few poems. There I really begin to get near what I was after.[6]

A crow is an intelligent, widely distributed and omnivorous bird, black, solitary, tough and unmusical; as an eater of carrion, it is dependant on death and destruction. It is a kind of digestive machine in flight. All these attributes are present in Hughes's bird,

but they are subordinated by the apocalyptic context in which it
turns up in the cycle, suspiciously close, as I've said, to the Christian
tradition, for all Hughes's radical doubts and undermining views,
and in particular the familiar Biblical account of the history of the
world and humanity's place in it, from beginning to end.

Hughes splendidly anticipated this development in a few poems
in *Wodwo*, for instance 'Theology' (p. 92) in which a humorous
and startling reversal of the Fall, emphasising digestion ('This is the
dark intestine') and God's ineffectiveness, anticipates the *Crow*
poems. Yet in *Crow*, what we have is much more powerful,
frightening and painful, as well as comic, and this is primarily
because of the unifying presence of the Crow itself, which is
fundamentally a metaphor but one extended by its use in so many
different contexts so that it becomes mythical.

We've already looked at Crow's new account of the Fall, in 'A
Childish Prank' (*SP*, p. 116), but before Crow even enters the
world, he faces a catechism, or 'Examination at the Womb Door',
which tells us a lot about him (see p. 115):

> Who owns these scrawny litle feet? Death.
> Who owns this bristly scorched-looking face? Death.
> Who owns these still-working lungs? Death.
> Who owns this utility coat of muscles? Death.
> Who owns these unspeakable guts? Death...

And so on, until

> But who is stronger than death?

> Me, evidently.

Pass, Crow.

With brilliant timing, the poem reveals that on one level, Crow *is*
just a cocky, humorous, tough, *surviving* voice, that defeats even
death. Amazingly, absurdly, Crow (and therefore humanity) can
survive everything. This is the miracle the *Crow* poems celebrate.
Inevitably, in our time, and with our knowledge of what we are
capable of, this is a miracle with a dark underside — as the
violence, fear and terror of many of the poems makes shockingly
clear. 'As flies to wanton boys are we to the gods' (*King Lear*, IV, i,
line 36), here, you might say; but, as in *King Lear's* chaotic
universe, there is also (if in an even more questionable, attenuated
form) the possibility of meaning, order and survival.

Yet — what *is* our place, exactly, in the *Crow* universe? God has little to do with his creation, it seems, so it's not too surprising that when he finds himself confronted by Adam and Eve, he is at a loss to know how to give them some kind of purposeful activity. So Crow comes to his aid. He has only just been born, and it's his first 'Childish Prank' on old God. You will recall the last lines of that sardonic little poem:

> Man awoke being dragged across the grass.
> Woman awoke to see him coming.
> Neither knew what had happened.
>
> God went on sleeping.
>
> Crow went on laughing.

Christianity, claims Hughes, is 'just another provisional myth of man's relationship with the creator'; and the God of *Crow* he calls the 'man-created, broken-down, corrupt despot of [this] ramshackle religion who bears about the same relationship to the creator as, say, ordinary English does to reality'.[7] Here he proposes another force, a force Christianity ignores, or pretends to ignore, or has forgotten. It is instinctual, animal, but shared by humankind and beast. It evolves willy-nilly, without any active intervention from God, as the poem 'Crow Tyrannosaurus' makes quite clear: from the animals up to man, there seems to be nothing but appetite. Crow has a flicker of conscience: 'Alas/Alas ought I/To stop eating/and try to become the light?' he thinks, 'But his eye saw a grub. And his head, trapsprung, stabbed.' The flicker is lost in the downward spiral of evolution. Yet it *was there*; and will reappear. Crow, in fact, shows fitful signs of becoming human, as the religious overtones make inevitable. He cannot remain mere animal, mere matter. He even becomes aware of good and evil. Where is that evil? Read 'The Black Beast' (p. 119) and see if you can find an answer.

DISCUSSION

Like us, Crow would rather destroy everything than find evil where it really is — within ourselves. What about good? Crow, like everything else, continues to exist, so there must be something good, sustaining him — or must there? This is where theology starts. So Crow gives us his version, his theology (not in *SP*):

[*Crow's Theology*]

Crow realized God loved him -
Otherwise, he would have dropped dead.
So that was proved ...

he begins;

But what
Loved the stones and spoke stone? ...

since they, too, exist?

And what loved the shot-pellets
That dribbled from those strung-up mummifying crows?

Finally, comes the realisation that

there were two Gods —
One of them much bigger than the other
Loving his enemies
And having all the weapons.

Once again, what began to seem a hopeful, even optimistic view of
life, is sharply brought down. And in this vein, the poems continue:
look at 'Crow's First Lesson' (p. 117), 'Crow and the Birds' (p. 120)
and, again, 'Crow's Last Stand' (p. 127) as well as 'Notes for a
Little Play' (p. 130). That final poem leaves us with a last, appalling
image, of post-nuclear mutants dancing

... in the darkness of the sun,

Without guest or God.

What are we to think of this view of life? Perhaps you share the
reaction of such a critic as David Holbrook that this cannot
represent a sufficient, much less a full account of our shared
experience of life, and that Hughes has given himself over entirely
to the gods of hate and violence? Certainly there is much, much
more in the original collection to justify this view.[8] Or can we say
the sequence is, after all, *satire* and so, inevitably, as grimly
reductive, or horrifically nihilist, as satire can be — and, indeed,
often has been, from its primitive origins.

It is worth considering, for a moment, what those origins are. I am thinking less of the familiar medieval beast-epics such as *Reynard the Fox*, and their Classical (Aesopian) antecedants, than of the general, folkloric, oral roots of satire. Keith Sagar and others (including Hughes himself) have drawn attention to the similarities between the Crow-figure and the North American Winnebago Indian Trickster, a semi-divine creature who is driven out of society for breaking its taboos and sets off on a fantastic journey which leads to many absurd and often violent adventures of a generally anarchic, but especially sexual, kind.[9] This is helpful, but does rather leave the reader unread in anthropology with the impression that there still is not very much to be done about the nastier side of *Crow*. Yet, one of the sources for this kind of information, the anthropologist Paul Radin, has also pointed out that satire as such is conspicuous among all primitive societies, where it is used for everything from punishing bad behaviour to ritual cursing, but always with an aggressive and fantastic, as well as comic and entertaining intention.[10] This is surely familiar ground? Whether an Eskimo song, a couplet by Pope, a pamphlet by Swift, a children's playground rhyme, or a film by Chaplin, there is a very wide range of cultural forms and artefacts which may be said to exhibit the characteristics of satire, some of them at least familiar to everyone; and what they have in common is a militant, subversive urge which ensures precisely a one-sided view. There is no attempt to offer a comprehensive account of the human condition — that is not the point of satire. And Hughes is drawn to satire — whether he admits it or not — because of the bold clarity and simplicity, the directness, above all the violence of its usual manner, whether explicit or hidden, as it proceeds to undermine whatever is held sacred. Of course, as this suggests, satire depends for its effectiveness upon a context in which something *is* still held sacred, in which the myths, rituals and religions of the past are not entirely forgotten or unfamiliar; and this is true of the *Crow* sequence, whatever Hughes's ambitions towards 'a super-simple and super-ugly language'.

What we are offered in *Crow* then, is a critical, aggressive and humbling account of an insane world that is nonetheless recognisable, if only in terms of what it appears to reject or overturn. In this world, man is dominated by his own violence and sexuality: and I write 'man' here advisedly, since the Crow is evidently a male creature, genitaled thus in Baskin's drawings, referred to by the male pronoun (although also sometimes as 'it'), and behaving with an excess of brutality — typically beating 'the

hell' out of others ('A Horrible Religious Error', p. 121) — all too
easily identifiable with the dominant notion of masculinity in our
culture. It may be that this is sufficient to put off many among his
audience. It has been an aspect of Hughes's verse from the start, as
Keith Sagar admits, although he then justifies ignoring it on the
grounds that for Hughes to take seriously attacks upon his mindless
heroes 'would have been to emasculate himself',[11] which sounds
like special pleading indeed. But, I would argue, while nothing can
redeem the elements of admiring, overbearing machismo exposed
in some poems — from 'Macaw and Little Miss', 'where the
warrior comes, lightning and iron,/Smashing and burning and
rending towards her loin' (*The Hawk in the Rain*), to the ritual rape
and murder of 'Felicity' (in *Gaudete*) — there is also a recognition
elsewhere of the questionableness of all this: in, as I have suggested,
'Hawk Roosting', for example, but also in the *Crow* sequence itself.
This is partly a matter of structure. The most dark, the most
violent poems (in 'Crow's Account of St George' the hero is finally
'trousered in blood') are, after all, set within a series, which
concludes on the quietly accepting note of 'Two Eskimo Songs' and
'Littleblood' (p. 134). These calm the battered reader down again,
returning us to the everyday in a kind of peace. But, this is also a
matter of admitting and responding to the mythical dimension
within individual poems.

Thus, for example, there is 'The Contender' (pp. 123–4), one of
a number of poems which appear to be by, rather than about,
Crow. Is is merely a celebration of big-chested masculine heroism,
as the title and opening lines suggests? Or, if we keep in mind the
idea that this is exaggerated, militant satire, does it perhaps rework
a familiar mythical-religious event so as to question the 'heroism'
formerly associated with it?

DISCUSSION

> There was this man and he was the strongest
> Of the strong ...

I read this as light-hearted parody, even as it suggests that what we
are about to hear is an epic tale of the exploits of a massive male
figure, a 'contender'. 'All the women in the world could not move
him', seems to confirm this reading. But then, as we read on, we
realise that the hero is already dead, and, as the satiric
exaggerations expand ('He gritted his teeth like a cliff'), the
fantasy-horror grows ('Grinning through his atoms and decay'),

and the mythical-religious overtones accumulate, ('nailed', then 'crucified') we realise that this is Christ; or, at least, a version of Christ as a dead, male hero-figure. The 'heroic' opening has become a darkly comic, absurd beginning to a 'tale' that ends with a forlorn image of the Christian saviour, transformed into a mere skull upon the earth,

> Grinning into the black
> Into the ringing nothing
> Through the bones of his teeth
>
> Sometimes with eyes closed
>
> In his senseless trial of strength.

The last phrase recalls the opening, thereby enclosing this unheroic, subversive view of the Christian god-man within pseudo-epic formulae. If Christ, or Man-as-god, can be promoted in terms of masculine heroism, it is only to underline the figure's sterility and pointlessness, now. This is bound to be offensive to many believing Christians, if not also to others who lean on the Christian tradition and its central, worshipped man. But it is quite a different matter from criticising such poems for their 'mindless violence'.

Where there may be more of a problem is in the use of less apparently familiar, long-standing myths: for instance, in the Crow version of Freud's Oedipal interpretation of sexuality, offered as a gruesome nursery rhyme entitled 'Song for a Phallus', which begins

> There was a boy was Oedipus
> Stuck in his Mammy's belly
> His Daddy'd walled the exit up
> He was a horrible fella
>
>   Mamma Mamma

and ends:

> He split his Mammy like a melon
> He was drenched with gore
> He found himself curled up inside
> As if he had never been bore
>
>   Mamma Mamma

The Oedipus legend, as it is reworked here, lacks the mythical weight (and challenge) which centuries of Christianity can provide elsewhere in *Crow*, and which therefore provide a workable context to the extreme, 'violent' image of so much of the sequence. On the other hand, the view of sexuality implied in this 'Song', in which life and death, creation and destruction, are super-imposed upon one another, may also be said to be, ultimately, grounded in that same long, religious tradition, which, for some readers, could make such a poem the more powerfully subversive. But, then, look at the two 'love poems' 'Lovesong' (pp. 128–9) and 'The Lovepet' (pp. 131–2, taken from *Moortown*), in which the lovers become one another, or become their joint desires. Are not these, for all their surreality, monotonous and banal? To my mind, the rather facile tendency of such poems ('He loved her and she loved him … In the morning they wore each other's face', and so on) prevents them working successfully, and it is a tendency which, unfortunately, surfaces in more and more of the poetry of the *Crow* period, not excluding some of the *Crow* poems themselves. 'Crow's First Lesson' (p. 117) is another example, which you have only to read together with its immediate predecessor (in the original, and in *Selected Poems*, pp. 116–7), 'A Childish Prank', to recognise how directness can become crudity, and cosmic humour, facile absurdity. Or so it seems to me; you must read the poems and decide for yourself, in the end. With poetry of this kind, rude, extreme and ungracious, readers are bound to divide strongly, and exactly where they divide, which poems remain 'readable' or, if you like, 'acceptable', is something that is going to be more than usually difficult to predict or determine.

What remains important, however, is the overriding sense in *Crow* that even the excessive and banal form part of an overall vision — cumulative, daring and foolish, but unignorable. The strongest and most persuasive aspect of this, it seems to me, is that drawn from the old and familiar Biblical myths. There's no redeemer in this vision (in 'The Contender', he could not be more finally dead), and only once do we come near the possibility, with both nasty and comic results, in 'Crow Blacker than ever':

> When God, disgusted with man,
> Turned towards heaven
> And man, disgusted with God,
> Turned towards Eve,
> Things looked like falling apart.

Then Crow nails everyone and everything together, until 'the joint' stinks, a 'horror beyond redemption'. The last word alerts us to the possibility inherent in it. Crow just grins, crying 'This is my Creation', and is left 'Flying the black flag of himself'. That grin is typical: it is the essence of satire, the death's head grin of fear and despair, which nevertheless implies survival, because it is there. And, perhaps also, redemption? The unrelenting humour, which can turn even the arrival of sin and death into a wonderfully funny 'Apple Tragedy' (p. 126), may seem to disallow any such hope. Yet, as the comparison with Lawrence in the preceding chapter showed, Hughes's dark nihilism does not exclude a certain revelatory, quasi-religious perception at the heart of things. Or, to take another comparison, like Vasko Popa, Hughes writes this poetry in the knowledge, as he says of Popa, that human politics have been 'weighed out in dead bodies by the million', and yet that 'man is also, at the same time and in the same circumstances, an acutely conscious human creature of suffering and hope', with 'doubtful and provisional senses, so indefinable as to be almost silly, but palpably existing, and wanting to go on existing'.[12]

This saving sense of humour and vitality which, willy-nilly, emerges from time to time in the *Crow* sequence, seems to have deserted Hughes entirely in the other large projects of the time, such as *Gaudete* (which means, of course, 'Rejoice', alluding to the birth of the Saviour). Finding failure, one looks for reasons, though these involve speculations which go beyond my scope here. It may be that, for example, Hughes's struggle to create meaning out of despair revived those childhood memories, of warscapes and chapel dogma, to an extent that his imagination was driven down some peculiarly obscure and unrewarding paths. How else to account for the confused and confusing verse/prose tale of the Yorkshireman at the centre of *Gaudete*, the Reverend Lumb (his name derived from Lumb Bank, near Hughes's birthplace), and the (on occasion) austerely beautiful, but largely impenetrable poems of *Cave Birds*, and *Earth Numb*? There is in any case insufficient specificity of reference and allusion to give purchase to any such explanation. Critics dredge through Hughes's own, frequently gnomic, utterances, they scrutinise myths familiar and unfamiliar — Graves's *The White Goddess* is still the most likely source of aid — but without very much conviction.[13] Courageously, or sensibly, depending on how you look at it, Hughes has only chosen a few of the obscurely bare, lyrical poems from the Epilogue of *Gaudete* for the *Selected Poems* (pp. 156–164). They do have a certain haunting eloquence, colloquial and distinctive: for example, the penultimate poem of the sequence, which draws us in to share a wondering responsiveness to nature by considering an ancient tree:

And my eyes pause
On the centuries of its instant

As gnats
Try to winter in its wrinkles.

We do not need to know that the tree which is this poem's
ostensible subject featured as the Reverend Lumb's ritual other self
near the beginning of his adventures, when he is flogged to
unconsciousness in its arms. We do not need to know this in order
to respond to an extraordinary evocation of timeless reality, a
massive, all-encompassing ability to survive, as nature survives:

The seas are thirsting
Towards the oak.

The oak is flying
Astride the earth.

With the calm, confident precision of a Japanese haiku, these lines
reveal a poet of vigorous affirmation, rather than bleak denial.

The paradox is only apparent: certain forms of modern art
require darkness in order to express themselves. In this way they
connect with our shared sense of estrangement, with our inability,
not merely unwillingness, to communicate. Some of the *Cave Birds*
poems, for all that they are mostly incomprehensible without their
attendant drawings by Baskin, (as Hughes admits: *SP*, Notes, p.
237) do provoke a vague, yet luminous fear, if I may so express it.
Abstract and generalised, excerpts from an inner drama (an
'Alchemical Cave Drama' concerning innocence, guilt and heroic
rebirth), they nevertheless touch on deep, obscurely powerful
feelings. 'The Knight' (pp. 138–9) 'grows only more vast' as the
forces of nature 'squabble' to decompose his body, until nothing is
left but 'his weapons/And his gaze',

While hour by hour the sun
Strengthens its revelation.

The medieval trappings do not fool us: the revelation is
subliminally connected with that nuclear glare which revealed us to
ourselves as mutants, staggering on, in 'Notes for a Little Play'.
There is only one drama here, and it is familiar, unpleasantly,
horribly familiar. Yet Hughes exploits the ambivalence of his own
continuing utterance to suggest that we may hope for another day.

It is, I think, a mistake — although an easy one to make,

perhaps — to take the *Crow* cycle as merely violent and nihilistic. The very use of myths, even overturned ones, implies a struggle to find meaning in life, if not order and complete understanding. We must face the worst in ourselves, the Black Beast, Hughes says. But the beast is *our* creation, like Crow, God, humanity; and so we *can* alter it. How? He offers no answer. But, like the so-called 'Littleblood' of the very last poem, 'drumming in a cow's skull/Dancing with a gnat's feet', if we have 'Grown ... wise ... [and] terrible', knowing death awaits us, perhaps we *can* also 'sing'.

7. Back to Mother Nature

The problem for many of Ted Hughes's readers and critics is that the persistent awareness of forces 'out there' which makes his work so powerful seems at times exclusively an awareness of the terrible destructiveness in things — which, apparently, he welcomes. There can be little doubt of the loud, battering-ram effect of certain poems, such as the title poem of *The Hawk in the Rain*; and that timidity gets attacked, as in 'Famous Poet', a blustering satiric complaint against those who lack the 'vital fire' (p. 16) required by poetry today; and that other poems, such as 'Egg-Head' or 'The Man Seeking Experience Enquires His Way of a Drop of Water' (pp. 23–6), broaden the attack to include anyone who might avoid the testing extremes of feeling we are supposed to face. Telling us this in a loud voice is, of course, no substitute for making us feel it, and it may be that we can dismiss such poems as mere rhetoric. After all, in later poems such as 'Hawk Roosting' or 'Ghost Crabs', Hughes allows us both to respond to and control, such feelings; and, in the *Crow* sequence at least, brutality and bloodshed may be understood in relation to the larger vision of which they are an important part.

Nevertheless, Hughes himself has kept the more ferocious *Crow* poems out of the *Selected Poems*, along with most of the butcheries of *Gaudete*, which go on 'Till blood drips from the mouth' (p. 159, from the Epilogue). Yet among what remains, there is the crude physicality of *Seven Dungeon Songs* (e.g., pp. 221–4); and, indeed, the damning 'Tiger Psalm', from *Earth-Numb* (pp. 227–8), which celebrates the whole underlying philosophy implicit in the idea that 'The tiger blesses with a fang'.

There is no quick or easy counter to the view that there is an absence of compassion and humility, of humanity, about such poems. It is difficult to accept the defense that this is entirely a matter of exploring or acknowledging the apparent sources of Hughes's violence and extremism in the extravagant actions of folkloric, legendary or mythical creatures, especially when these are in practice exotic or unfamiliar. Indeed, such associations may only bear out the further contention that there is an element of dangerous nostalgia about Hughes's work, nostalgia for a lost or non-existent world of instinctual responses which is dangerous because it carries with it the authoritarian, chest-beating, 'macho' qualities most liable in the end to bring about the mass destruction envisaged by, say, 'Notes for a Little Play'. Dangerous, too, because it is so seductive, most of all when handled with the blithe wit embodied in a creature like 'Esther's Tomcat', who 'grallochs odd dogs on the quiet' and whose behaviour is likened to the sharp splendours of feudal combat (p. 41: 'grallochs' being a nicely archaic Gaelic word for disembowelling).

Does this mean, then, that we should agree, for instance, with Martin Dodsworth, who finds Hughes 'radically flawed' as a poet on account of his 'inability to come to terms with the cruelty and destructiveness' expressed in so many of his poems?[1] Maybe we should. But I am not totally convinced, yet. For one thing, this leaves out too much: of what we know about the context and perspective in which Hughes may be viewed and, even more compelling, of his actual, and some of his finest, poetry. In this chapter, I will explore this a little further, by suggesting not only what Hughes himself has argued in his own defense, but also by looking at a group of poems so far untouched (and virtually ignored by those who follow Dodsworth's line), from *Season Songs* (1976) *Remains of Elmet*, (1979), *Moortown*, (1979) and *River* (1983). It would be helpful if you now read through the poems from these collections reprinted in *Selected Poems*.

Consider this passage:

> I write about violence as naturally as Jane Austen wrote about manners. Violence shapes and obsesses our society, and if we do not stop being violent we have no future. People who do not want writers to write about violence want to stop them writing about us and our time. It would be immoral not to write about violence.

No, this is not by Hughes: but by the playwright, Edward Bond.[2] Of course, it begs a number of questons, such as *how* the writer of today deals with violence. But my point is, Hughes is not alone in his obsession, far from it; nor should we expect him to be.

However, unlike Edward Bond, and others who go on to identify the violence they perceive with a specific, historical and social structure, Hughes locates it nowhere — and everywhere, as a universal, natural force. 'My poems are not about violence but vitality'. Pressed later to explain this further, he said: 'Any form of violence — and form of vehement activity — invokes the bigger energy, the elemental power circuit of the Universe'. For Hughes, the sheer vitality of primal nature, animal and human, has had to take the place of God. How is this energy to be tapped and controlled? By means of ritual, 'the machinery of religion'.[3] Since Christianity is no longer available, or at least is disintegrating so fast we cannot rely upon its traditional strengths, other structures of belief, other myths, must be created, or recreated. And it is the poet's task to do this. If there is an historical, social dimension, it is evidently secondary.

Only occasionally is there an explicit connection between Hughes's poems and the times we live in, and, where there is, it usually fails to work on any level beyond the most superficial. In 'A Woman Unconscious', for example (p. 38), the familiar 'animalising' metaphoric transformation of the subject is stale and predictable: 'Russia and America circle each other' like two animals preparing to fight. Their threats to cancel the world out in a nuclear holocaust render the possibility of change meaningless. We have to realise

> That the future's no calamitous change
> But a malingering of now,
> Histories, towns, faces that no
> Malice or accident much derange.

In other words, there has been history, but it has become 'now', the immediate moment, forever. And what is this moment in the poem? The private death revealed in the last stanza: no 'lesser death' for the perceiving individual than 'Earth gone in an instant flare'.

Perhaps not. But what this suggests is that personal and public are indistinguishable; and time, as history, exists only in the present.

To my mind, this is only persuasive in so far as it is a response to the private death the poem is ostensibly about; not as a response to the times we live in. 'Woman Unconscious' (which dates from the late fifties) reveals one clear limit to Hughes's imagination: dealing with public, social, historical reality is quite beyond him. This may also be symptomatic: of the 'fatalism and apathy, coming from the powerlessness of the individual', which G. S. Fraser identified as characterising the period beginning with the onset of the Cold War.[4] Hughes's 'war' poems, which go back to the First World War, may seem to be more aware of history and the possibility of change on account of their subject-material. But they are not: their interest is also doggedly personal, not only in the sense that the poems connect with a set of specific private memories, as we've seen, but also in the sense that they serve a static, inward vision. 'To Paint A Water Lily' perfectly illustrates this.

For Hughes, contemporary, like past, history is a 'red herring', as he observed of Eliot's *The Waste Land*; and

> Every writer if he develops at all develops either outwards into society and history, using wider and more material of that sort, or he develops inwards into imagination and beyond that into spirit, using perhaps no more external material than before and maybe even less but deepening it and making it operate in the many different inner dimensions until it opens up perhaps the religious or holy basis of the whole thing ....

T. S. Eliot went inward; Yeats managed to develop both outwardly and inwardly, so that his 'mythology is history, pretty well, and his history is as he said "the story of a soul"'.[5] Hughes himself may be said to follow Yeats — and Lawrence and Robert Graves — by attempting to mythologise the present and the past, and, like their common Romantic ancestors, by insisting that the earliest, most significant force in human history is the imagination. Like Blake,

> To cast off Bacon, Locke & Newton from Albion's covering,
> To take off his filthy garments & clothe him with Imagination,
> To cast aside from Poetry all that is not Inspiration

> (*Milton*, Book the Second)

is Hughes's aim. Like Blake, he tries to evoke the inner reality of primitive, instinctual energies which, he feels, are warped and obscured by our rational, social selves. He conceives of us as typically living in a state of alienation from our 'real' selves, muffled by sensible, everyday life from the violence and vitality which surge beneath. 'I have tried to suggest', he concluded his account of *Poetry in the Making*, 'how infinitely beyond our ordinary notions of what we know our real knowledge, the real facts for us, really is. And to live removed from this inner universe of experience is also to live removed from ourself, banished from ourself and real life'. According to Hughes, 'England lost her soul' between the middle of the sixteenth century and the middle of the seventeenth. What happened was that 'the gradual rise of Puritanism, together with its accompanying materialist and democratizing outlook and rational philosophy', suppressed 'the old goddess', Nature. Shakespeare's poetry, like all great poetry, tries to help 'redress' the 'balance' of forces in the universe, upset by such 'human error'.[6] We need to go back to 'the old goddess', Nature, if we are truly, that is, imaginatively, spiritually, to find ourselves.

Of course, Hughes's emphasis, and manner, are modern: he attempts to create out of the collapse of all traditional forms and values a new vision, which simultaneously admits what we have done to our selves, and may yet do. In poem after poem, the strange but vital otherness of the imagination is revealed, acting with the power of vision, to penetrate the secret lairs of the mind. You will remember 'The Thought-Fox': please re-read it now. Having become familiar with so much of Hughes's work and his approach you may find that it takes on a further, but inward, dimension. Think about the line, 'Through the window I see no star'. What does it suggest? It seems to indicate a void, an absence waiting to be filled. Will it be? In that bizarre and memorable, Blakean opening, which yoked together the abstract 'moment' with the concrete 'forest', a vague 'something' was alive, as if waiting ... and then this rather nightmarish 'something' emerged, gradually, uncertainly, until it became a 'bold' body, an 'eye', focusing what is happening until, with that 'sudden sharp hot stink of fox' the dark interior of the head was filled — a climax with curiously unpleasant overtones. This is when we realise that the imagination at work can be a subversive, even threatening, power, an idea reinforced in the poem by the image it conveys of one's head as the secret lair of a predatory animal. That the window remains starless, brings out the essentially inward and solitary nature of the whole process, which can now be understood to undermine the apparent clinching certainty of the last line: the page is printed, yes, but forces have been realised, or at least hinted at, which are not so easily captured or controlled.

For all these reasons, Hughes maintained a tenacious grip upon the poetry of packed, detailed, natural observation even through the time of writing *Crow*, *Cave Birds* and *Gaudete*, as if oblivious of their large and often horrifying implications. In effect what he was doing, was taking us back to the goddess Nature: the aggressive, masculine, satiric view so forcibly embodied in these sequences is countered by a lighter, gentler and more feminine strain, which emerges with the publication of *Season Songs* — some of which had actually appeared before *Cave Birds*, and the nucleus of which pre-dated the first publication (but not all the writing) of *Crow*. It is vital for a proper understanding of Hughes's poetry to realise that these aspects of his writing were coterminous, and why.

You might well feel uncomfortable with the notions of 'masculine' and 'feminine' that I have proposed here. Certainly you will if you are at all familiar with the feminist movement in general or feminist literary theory in particular. This is not the place, nor do I have the space, even supposing I were able, to explore what might be considered a feminist approach to Hughes's work, although I am sure that such an approach is long overdue.[7] I suspect that many feminists, if not women readers in general, would consider Hughes's attitude and work irredeemably 'phallocentric': not only, perhaps, because of the emphasis upon violence (although, as I have tried to suggest, that is better understood as an emphasis upon energy and power); but also because of his overt obsession with male hero figures, creatures which, whether animal or human, seem invariably domineering, not to say brutal and predatory. Battle, too, must seem an obsession typically male. But while it is broadly true that Hughes's vision is 'masculine', that does not simply mean it should be ignored or can be so very easily dismissed. For one thing, if our current situation is as bad as it is because of the patriarchal inheritance, the inheritance of a culture dominated by certain 'masculine' attributes, then it is surely necessary at the least to try and understand those attributes and their cultural consumption. This means, in Hughes's case, to respond to as well as to analyse (true analysis involves a response) the feelings and meanings his work mediates so persuasively. It also involves recognising the importance for his poetry — however subjective and unhistorical a view it may be — of the notion that the female principle in nature has been suppressed, with the consequent need now for its recuperation. This notion appears from very early on — perhaps even underlies the early, Gravesian 'Song' with its concluding lament, 'O lady, consider when I shall have lost you ...' (p. 14). Hughes seems to have taken in from the start a belief in the white goddess representing some basic matriarchal urge in nature which was, once, dominant, yet which has long been suppressed (Graves thinks by the Greek classical mythologists). On the other hand, there is also throughout Hughes's work a continuing assumption of a kind of biological determinism which is viewed almost entirely in its male aspect — in all those predatory creatures which we are invited to take as crucially representative of the human psyche, but also, and more explicitly, in later poems such as 'Life is Trying to be Life'. Here the poet attempts precisely to suggest the shape of the most basic, underlying qualities of being, and the poem, from *Earth-Numb* (reprinted in *Moortown* and *SP*, pp. 217–8), begins with an image of the inextricability of death in life, which is imagined as 'Death is in the sperm like the ancient mariner/With his horrible tale'. The pun on 'tale' doesn't help much: this seems an absurdity, however you read it. But even if we take it that this expresses the deathly element in the male, rather than a presumption that the life force can only be imagined in such male terms (and elsewhere Hughes refers to 'the optimism of the sperm, still struggling joyfully along after 150 millions years'),[8] the giveaway comes later, when we are presented with a 'cave-wife' with her 'needle of bone'. Yes, she would be *sewing*, back in the cave, wouldn't she? Even more predictable than the caring, yet secondary figure thus represented, are the threatening overtones also connected with her, her needle suggesting in the next line a 'shark's fang'.

But there is a less stereotyped, more creative aspect to the feminine principle, as it appears in Hughes's later work. Referring, again, to his version of English history by way of Shakespeare, Hughes has proposed a contemporary fable, drawn from two characters in *The Tempest*, and written originally as 'Crow's Song about Prospero and Sycorax', which then became one of the 'Orts' or scraps of *Moortown*, before being republished in the *Selected Poems* (p. 226): this is 'Prospero and Sycovax'.

I would like you to read 'Prospero and Sycorax' now, in conjunction with Hughes's 'Note' to his *Choice of Shakespeare's Verse*, to which I have already referred. 'She' is 'Sycorax' from *The Tempest*, Caliban's witch-mother, who is supposedly brought under control by Prospero's magic powers. Here, the 'Shakespearian fable' identifies the banishment of the life-giving, sensual, female urge, whose 'knowledge' resides in an awareness of all that is lost with the loss of her power by her enslavement to the male. It may well be no coincidence that Hughes placed this on the page opposite 'Tiger-Psalm' in the *Selected Poems* (p. 227): certainly it puts the latter into perspective, whether or not one is able to accept the mythical, inward version of history on which it is based.

All of this, I would suggest, helps us see what is happening in the apparent 'turn' to the 'feminine' in *Season Songs* — and, indeed, much of Hughes's work subsequently. It is not just a question of recognising the point and purpose of, say, 'The River in March' being imagined as a woman, or the spring air in 'April Birthday'

> Lifting through all the
> Gently-breasted counties of England

before

> A shiver of green
> Strokes the darkening slope as the land
> Begins her labour

The delightful, vividly sensual celebration of the goddess Nature in *Season Songs* has led to them being called simply the 'reverse image of *Crow's* showy toughness and attitudinising', merely an 'affected, winsome prettiness, verging on the prissy flutterings of an old maid'.[9] Hughes's work cannot be blamed for the sexism of some of his critics, I trust. The remark was, in fact, called forth by 'April Birthday', a poem in any case not one of the more persuasive or moving of these contained in the collection — which even a quick glance at the three in *Selected Poems* (pp. 143–7) should substantiate. As it happens, *Crow's* 'showy toughness' is also 'proved' by one of the weakest examples from that sequence, one, again, not included in Hughes's own selection: 'Crow's Account of St. George'. Such simplistic contrasts are common and involve a misreading of both books of poems, as well as a lack of attention to what we know Hughes has said elsewhere, in verse and prose. As I have tried to argue, while it is subject to flaws, *Crow* is also part of a larger vision which implies the possibility of struggling through, of surviving, in the face of the worst. 'Two Eskimo Songs' show this, as do other poems which stress the continuity of life implicit in the venture, the singing, itself — such as 'Owl's Song' (p. 122).

It is striking that some of the *Season Songs* are written in the Crow 'style': 'There Came a Day' opens

> There came a day that caught the summer
> Wrung its neck
> Plucked it
> And ate it.

Arbitrary, bare, 'violent' — and comic, in that characteristically surreal, primitive manner. Crow himself makes an appearance in one poem, 'Leaves', based upon the familiar nursery-rhyme pattern of 'Cock Robin', each stanza starting with a question: 'Who's killed the leaves?/Me, says the apple ...', 'Who sees them drop? / Me, says the pear...', and so on until

> Who'll be their parson?
> Me, says the Crow, for it is well-known
> I study the bible right down to the bone.
> I'll be their parson.

But the overriding impression is one of *energy*: of the stunning power of nature, variously embodied in the processes of the seasons, and the creatures that share it. In 'Swifts', which begins with a wonderful evocation of the power of flight, the birds materialise out of nowhere,

> at the tip of a long scream
> Of needle. "Look! They're back! Look!" And they're gone
> On a steep
>
> Controlled scream of skid
> Round the house-end and away under the cherries.
>
> (p. 146)

The beautifully judged, freewheeling lines and stanzas mimic an intense reality, which accumulates beneath the poem's cheerfully anecdotal domestic surface, until we arrive at the death and burial of one tiny bird, 'my little Apollo', which is yet not the end of the poem, where we are left with

> The charred scream
> Folded in its hugh power.
>
> (p. 147)

Is this 'winsome' or 'prissy'? Hardly. We are back to the larger dimension, to the immense, apparently unfeeling and relentless forces of nature, the 'energy-circuit' of the universe. Yet these forces have been identified within a recognisable, indeed gently English landscape, suggestively female.

It is tempting to connect this turn with a return, a return to personal roots. The temptation is encouraged by *Remains of Elmet* in which, as we have seen, Hughes memorialises his familiar, family landscape. The collection begins with the dedication: 'Poems in Memory of Edith Farrar', Hughes's mother; and opens with this plunge into the past from the present,

> Six years into her posthumous life
> My uncle raises my Mother's face
> And says Yes he would love a cup of tea.

The personal, domestic and familiar apparently tug the poet back, *'strange depths'* coming alive, because *'attached to me'*. *'And the smoky valley opens, the womb that bore him'*. *Remains of Elmet*, a sequence of haunting poems amplified by Fay Godwin's stark accompanying photographs of Hughes's home valley, begins and ends with an evocation of the womanly, maternal forces in nature. The penultimate poem, 'Heptonstall Cemetery' (p. 181), itemises the poet's personal attachements (which include Sylvia Plath), as it suggests their immortalisation, with a calm gravity reminiscent of the 'Lucy' poems: the wind over the graveyard is like a great bird,

> And Thomas and Walter and Edith
> Are living feathers
>
> Esther and Sylvia
> Living feathers
>
> Where all the horizons lift wings
> A family of dark swans
> And go beating low through storm-silver
> Toward the Atlantic.

But there is finally no simple reassurance. The last poem ('The Angel') reveals a prophetic but terrifying mother-figure, whose presence leaves the metamorphosis of human into natural a powerful enigma.

The meaning of what is happening to him, in responding to the obscure powers evoked by contemplating his personal landscape, to the 'the harvest of long cemeteries' ('Walls'), seems to elude Hughes. What finally emerges from *Remains of Elmet*, is perhaps most dramatically revealed by 'Football at Slack', rather than by attempts to explore the maternal presence (as in 'Where The Mothers' or 'The Big Animal Of Rock'). 'Football at Slack' (p. 177) is, as its title suggests, primarily an account of a local game of football. It is a gently humorous, yet characteristically Hughesian piece which suddenly subverts its own domestic, everyday surface:

But the wingers leapt, they bicycled in the air
And the goalie flew horizontal

And once again a golden holocaust
Lifted the cloud's edge, to watch them.

'Once again', indeed: could it be that, while the familiar visionary awareness of the elemental forces at work in nature continues to hold us, it is a little too easily come by, now? Nevertheless, this 'holocaust', seen in a homely, human perspective suddenly opening up, needs to be set beside the holocaust of *Crow*, for a proper understanding of Hughes's complexity and ambivalence.

The warm responsiveness to the human, because known and personal, in *Remains of Elmet* finds richer and more persuasive expression in the 'Moortown Elegies'. The 'feminine' aspect of Hughes's vision may be understood as embodied in the continuing emphasis upon nature as creative, rather than destructive, apparent in the series of birth poems at the centre of this sequence. Birth and death are, as always, closely identified; but there is a rapt intensity, an almost sacramental attention to the mundane, physical detail of animal husbandry in these poems which implies a redeeming, or at least hopeful, perspective. The series began as part of a verse farming diary Hughes kept for a while, some of which was reprinted in Michael Morpurgo's *All Around The Year* (1979), an illustrated prose-and-poetry farming diary in which notes on lamb-ringing, sheep scab, fluke and the price of cows jostle happily with Hughes's poems. It provides a useful adjunct to the 'Elegies'. Any expectation that writing about domestic, farm animals, and not the wild predators of his earlier poetry, should produce a tamer, less 'violent' or 'brutal' view of life, is quickly defeated. 'February 17th', for example (pp. 191–2), about what happens when a lamb is too large for the mother bearing it, provides a harrowing description of precisely what is involved when one of nature's accidents takes place:

I caught her with a rope. Laid her, head uphill
And examined the lamb. A blood-ball swollen
Tight in its black felt, its mouth gap
Squashed crooked, tongue stuck out, black-purple,
Strangled by its mother.

Human intervention succeeds in releasing the small, pathetic corpse,

In a smoking slither of oils and soups and syrups —
And the body lay born, beside the hacked-off head.

Rarely has Hughes's ability to deploy the resources of an active, physical and urgent language been so brilliantly displayed, and to such apparently modest ends. Surely 'violence' and 'brutality' are the wrong words, for this? The death of the lamb in any case ensures the continuing life of its mother, who will bear other lambs.

We are invited to share these unsentimental, direct and unmoralised accounts of rural life — an invitation I find irresistible, because of the manner in which it is offered. A poem which confirms the sane certainty of the whole enterprise, and which can valuably be read alongside 'February 17th', tells of the successful birth of a calf. It is touching in its simple strength and, again, suggests the affirmative side to Hughes's vision. 'Birth of Rainbow' (pp. 185–6) opens on a typically packed, dense and powerful evocation of the natural scene:

> This morning blue vast clarity of March sky
> But a blustery violence of air, and a soaked overnight
> Newpainted look to the world.

'Violence' means energy, the 'energy-circuit' of the universe, but tied down by such specific detail to an immediately recognisable situation, there is nothing portentous about it. The poem then moves on to another detailed account of the actual event, the birth, followed by a suggestive opening-out into the 'whole South-West', then 'the world', which disappears

> in forty-five degree hail
> And a gate-jerking blast. We got to cover.
> Left to God the calf and his mother.

No need to make explicit the implication of the rainbow which provides the calf with its name, and the poem its title: signifying the promise of a relationship between God and humankind, through nature.

As Craig Robinson has pointed out in an excellent extended essay on the 'Moortown' sequence, the crucial added dimension to Hughes's exploration of our troubled relationship with nature here is the presence of the farmer: a real, practical presence, derived from the poet's own growing involvement in farm life in Devon, as well as his wish to memorialise his deceased partner and father-in-law, Jack Orchard (see, again 'Now You have to Push', referred to in Chapter 3, and 'The Formal Auctioneer', pp. 198–9). The 'rationale of farming', Robinson suggests, adds an integrating perspective to what might otherwise seem a relatively narrow choice of subject — bringing together the spiritual quest apparent in Hughes's mythic sequences, with his perceptive responsiveness to the processes of nature. If in his previous poetry, the natural and the human have too often been separate, 'it is the farm, par excellence', where the two meet.

> And the meeting is not a confrontation, since the farm can be seen as a working laboratory of co-operation between man and nature. Hughes has discovered in these poems the utility of a real situation perfectly apt for expressing ecological awareness, the sanctity of nature, and the value of man's being in touch with natural energies.[10]

In this way the poet's abiding theme, of the presence of amoral, primitive forces at work beneath the surface of our predominantly urban, 'civilised' culture, can be realised without the strain too often apparent in his earlier work, or the portentousness of his myth-sequences. It is no coincidence that in his public role he has allied himself with the conservationist movement — for instance, becoming 'embroiled in a fine old row about the decidedly unlyrical problem of sewage' in the River Torridge estuary at Bideford in Devon.[11] Or that he should also have taken an active interest in creative writing courses by supporting the Arvon Foundation's Devon centre, Totleigh Barton, since 1971, and by offering for its use his own house, Lumb Bank, near Heptonstall, since 1975: both centres set amidst the rural world he knows so well. Such practical activities represent an extension into the social, everyday world of Hughes's overriding concern to encourage the sense that we must return to the revivifying resources of nature — nature not in the abstract merely, but in the known world of our own environment. It is evident, too, that his willingness to serve as Poet Laureate is a part of how he sees his role in this respect — agreeing to publicise the opening of a new reservoir for fishing with the same alacrity that he helps celebrate the Queen Mother's eightieth birthday. His cultural position has become, then, appropriate, just as the bleak, despairing note sounded in so much of his work has been replaced by a lighter, more warmly humane, if sometimes rather 'occasional' and superficial tone.

This development has, in itself, affected Hughes's poetry, not least by its impact upon the production of his work. *River*, for example, a series of poems begun after a fishing expedition in Alaska with his son, became, 'with the assistance of British Gas and the Countryside Commission', a lush and expensive book of alternate poems and colour photographs (by Peter Keen). A happy

cause is, presumably, served; but several of the poems seem barely
worth a glance as accompaniments to the (admittedly superb)
photographs. What is most striking about the series is, as the poet
Peter Redgrove noticed when it first appeared, its emphasis upon
the 'relenting and feminine aspects of nature'. Redgrove linked this
femaleness with 'the willing sacrifice, the softness of the water of
the Tao, which, yielding to everything, conquers everything', and
instanced the title-poem, in which 'Fallen from heaven', the river
'lies across / The lap of his mother, broken by world', scattered and
buried, yet finally, 'a god, and inviolable. / Immortal. And will
wash itself of all deaths'.[12] Certainly there is a religious aura about
this, and several of the other poems, which may indeed derive from
Hughes's known interest in Eastern quietist philosophy;[13] but it is
also and more obviously a celebration of that all-embracing,
powerfully fecund nature goddess apparent in other poetry of this
phase in Hughes's career. Natural description, sexuality and
spirituality at times create an almost chaotic, uncontrolled writing,
as in 'Salmon Eggs', (pp. 232–3) which begins with the salmon 'just
down there —/ Shuddering together, caressing each other' then goes
on to see the river's bedrock below them,

And this is the liturgy
Of the earth's tidings — harrowing, crowned — a travail
Of raptures and rendings

Sanctus Sanctus

Swathes the blessed issue.

Perpetual mass

Of the waters
Wells from the cleft.

It is the raw vent

Of the nameless
Teeming inside atoms — and inside the haze
And inside the sun and inside the earth.

It is the font, brimming with touch and whisper,

Swaddling the egg.

Only birth matters

Say the river's whorls.

There is, is there not, something of a struggle going on here: to express the inexpressible, perhaps?

But the poet's job is to find a language that enables readers to go along the chosen way, however obscure and exploratory. In Hughes's work, tentativeness appears as a tendency to exaggerate and overstate, to lose himself in rhetorical expostulation. But the healing, the redeeming aim here should be clear enough. If we are to appreciate fully Hughes's return to mother nature, it is probably better to look for the quieter, more controlled response. The richest, most splendidly achieved example of what Hughes continues to be capable of in this respect, he has himself taken out of the *River* volume and placed as the last of his *Selected Poems*. Please read 'That Morning' now. Do you see how it absorbs and reaffirms his preoccupations? It goes back to the powerfully concentrated, yet disciplined evocation of a creature in its nonhuman environment (the salmon in the river)' reactivating a specific, personal memory of history and landscape (Lancasters over Yorkshire), and yet finally offers out of this encounter with primeval nature, the possibility of redemption, not destruction.

8. Conclusion

Hughes's belief in himself as bard is everywhere apparent in his work. This is more than merely a matter of having confidence in himself as a writer. It has to do with the primitive notion of 'shaman', to which he sometimes refers. The shaman is the visionary whose function it is to explore the spiritual unconscious of society on our behalf. To accept this view uncritically does not help anyone. For one thing, it means dodging the whole question of how his more mythic verse may reach those unfamiliar with, or unsympathetic towards, the often (but not always) obscure structures of belief upon which it draws. For another, it involves an arrogant presumption that this poet, and his poetry, provide the one path to enlightenment available to us. Only acolytes can go so far, and this book has not been addressed to them.

Yet, as should be clear even only on the basis of the relatively few poems I have been able to look at in any detail here, Hughes is undeniably a surprising, powerful and varied writer, who creates memorable and disturbing poetry, justifying its implicit claim for lastingness. Hughes himself has observed of 'The Thought-Fox' that 'everytime I read the poem the fox comes up again out of the darkness and steps into my head. And I suppose that long after I am gone, as long as a copy of the poem exists, every time anyone reads it the fox will get up somewhere out in the darkness and come walking towards them.'[1] That poem represented a fundamental discovery: of his role, and the nature of his work. This was more than a matter of finding out how well he could write about animals, although that was part of it. Only five of the poems in *The Hawk in the Rain* centred on animals; and the proportion did not increase much with the next two collections, *Lupercal* and *Wodwo*. Yet, as we have seen, the 'animal' poems did include much of the best in those early but definitive collections; and most of his poetry since them, apart from the explicitly 'war' poetry and *Gaudete*, has continued to focus upon the creaturely world, finding in it a continuing source of metaphor, symbol and myth.

In a recent book of prose and verse, *What is the Truth?* (1984), subtitled 'A Farmyard Fable For The Young', the figure of the fox reappeared, as if to prove Hughes's point. To begin with, in a near-domestic, farmyardly guise: then, again, mysterious, 'midnightish', apparently 'watching us'. 'It is', the narrator exclaims, 'a shock'. The creature's powerful, unexpected otherness is moving, as well as unpleasant, since we know he is about to be shot. But,

> Too deep in the magic wood, suddenly
> We have met the magician.

This gently ironic way of dealing with the force he has conjured up confirms Hughes's continuity, while it also suggests his development. The 'natural' imagery of his poetry of the sixties and seventies, from individual poems such as 'Ghost Crabs' to sequences such as *Crow*, may seem from a later perspective to have been excessively gloomy, pessimistic and loaded with atavistic horrors. But there has always been another, more humorous and humane, side — which, during the last decade, has made itself much more visible. And, as I have tried to show in the last chapter, even as we were plunged into the darker world of Crow, a lighter, mellower, more controlled, if still intensely vivid response to life was emerging: in *Season Songs*, the *Moortown Elegies* and *River*. This last book seems to have opened the way for the more recent works, such as *What is the Truth?* or *Flowers and Insects*, which concentrate upon the affirmative potential of the poet's final theme: the relation between ourselves and nature. The (masculine) urge to dominate and control our environment has been seen for what it is: a profoundly disturbing and ambivalent force, which may, now, require transforming into something altogether more respectful and accepting.

This much should suggest how far Hughes's position is from that of the simple, sentimental anthropomorphiser. He is still too often labelled an 'animal poet', although more often than not, by his detractors. But for all the sympathetic clarity with which his animals, birds or fishes are imagined, the poems have ultimately to do with human suffering, creativity and survival. If Hughes explores 'extreme' emotions in his poetry, he does so under the pressure of a vision which is constantly aware of the massive ebb and flow of natural forces underlying all life. With some important exceptions, he expresses the vision most successfully when dealing with the non-human world, at least on the surface, allowing the human implications to trickle in secretly, of their own accord. To see and appreciate this, we must read Hughes's work with real, but not uncritical attention; and we should read him whole. That is to say, including his verse for children, his 'fables for the young'.[2] We should also attend to his other writings, while keeping in mind the problems raised by relating the personal to the poetic.

I have assumed that the author's life and situation is a part of the reality with which his works engage; an assumption it is important to mention, because of recent attempts to undermine the traditional idea of the author — which is supposed to release us from assuming there is only one true or valid meaning to a text, generated by that author.[3] I prefer to suggest that it was in any case a dogmatic fantasy to suppose there ever was only one reading; that readers have always been fairly free about how they have interpreted what they have read; but that it is nevertheless very helpful to be reminded that the meanings of a poem are the product of *interaction* between writer, text and reader within particular situations; and that therefore Hughes's poems offer a wide (perhaps inexhaustible?) range of meanings, depending upon the changing circumstances of their consumption.

I have tried to keep this in mind, while believing that it is by being as clear as I can about what my approach involves that I make it easier for you to go your own way. In so far as I have been your guide, I have had to choose certain poems, and certain emphases, which I think provide the minimal access to Hughes's best work and to the world in which it operates. To begin with, this has meant looking at the most familiar, perhaps most obvious, poems and issues. But it has also meant that I have felt able, increasingly, to suggest my own views, and my own selection of the poetry which has provoked them. So perhaps, the best way to conclude, is to offer you some suggestions you might wish to pursue in quite other directions, from those which I have adopted here.

As you will have noticed, I have not dwelt upon Hughes's *Gaudete*, despite the very large claims some have made for it. One of those making such claims is Keith Sagar, whose approach to Hughes I have already suggested you should look at, if only because he provides so comprehensive a commentary, from so apparently privileged a position — knowing Hughes personally, and showing a close and long familiarity with all his works. Summing up his book on *The Art of Ted Hughes*, (p. 225) Sagar remarked:

> In so far as *Gaudete* can be said to have any progenitor in modern English literature, it is *The Waste Land*. Most of the great books and poems since then have been variations on its themes, new testimonies to the same social, cultural, psychological and spiritual conditions. Many writers have simply paraded their symptoms in the hope that they would turn out to be, as Eliot's were, or Kafka's, symptomatic of a whole culture. Some have offered a more conscious diagnosis. The few who have offered cures have been, in their very different ways, inadequate, doomed. There is a sense in which the great writers of this century have tended to cancel each other out. The orthodox religious/ mystical answers won't stand up. In *The Four Quartets* they are vacuous, the product of desperation and repudiation. Imagine a critique of it by Lawrence. The life-affirming answers have been too naive, taken too much for granted. Imagine a review of *Lady Chatterley's Lover* by Beckett. The nihilists and absurdists have allowed themselves the irresponsible luxury of despair. Imagine a review of *Waiting for Godot* by Brecht. The Marxists and meliorists have been so busy pulling up one bucket they have not noticed the other going down, nor the dead body in the well. Imagine a review of Brecht by Ionesco.
>
> Hughes is searching for a position which cannot be outflanked, which maintains human dignity and purpose without falsifying the facts, which recovers the same and the sacred without evasion, abstraction or doctrine. In *Gaudete* he has come close to achieving that.

Several critics have taken a more sceptical view. A good example is given by poet Peter Scupham in a review which takes as its starting-point *Moortown*, including a reading of 'February 17th' completely at odds with my own in the last chapter. The 'tenderness', says Scupham, 'and there is a great tenderness', he admits, about these poems,

> is overmatched by a kind of verbal assault and battery which deafens and can deaden the reader's response, as in 'February 17th', when in a parodic birth Hughes severs the head of a still-born lamb ... *Moortown* closes with a group of poems for the man with whom Hughes worked the land, and who becomes in his death a tenuous genius loci ... The poems in this initial sequence are both compulsive and infuriating. The sensitivity and vitality is undeniable, but there is a Lawrentian stridency; there is, too, a rape of the intellect which is disconcerting. This is due to the total lack of aesthetic distancing, the rejection of checks and balances, the even-handed intensity which equates all experiences. Leaves are mutilated, birds are fevered, hedges 'stand in coma', a raven curses: creation is caught in a web of multiplying verbal intensifiers. We must ride out the hurricane unquestioningly... The problem is that the experiences we are given are primary to Hughes, but the moment they are transposed into words they no longer hold the spontaneity they claim ... It could be argued that Hughes is, in a sense, writing on Active Service, and that the immediacy of these despatches from the front justifies their raw, unlicked quality ... [but] Hughes's lack of concern with the artifices of making displays a kind of arrogance which defeats criticism. We are presented constantly with the act of making, rather than the made: a wisdom that of the shaman rather than the poet. Hughes, like Fortuna, turns his restless wheel of reiterative births and deaths, stars and space, egos and alter-egos. Myths build and die; the natural world is substantial yet evanescent. Can the dictates of the subconscious supplant the reflection, the delays necessary to complete a work of art?[4]

A more suggestive and complex approach, yet nevertheless equally sceptical of Hughes's claims, might be one based upon a broader cultural perspective which admits that Hughes's readership is not limited to that England his poetry seems most concerned to address, but which also takes in the rich and various strands of the whole English-speaking world.

Thus, John Lucas has recently drawn attention to some remarks from an essay suggesting some of the ways in which Indians look at

English poetry since the war, including Hughes (this was written before John Betjeman died and Hughes replaced him as Laureate):

> Indisputably the loss of the jewel in her crown was a traumatic experience for Great Britain. We can show that this resulted in an insecure, an embattled, mental condition which in turn led writers to become more and more insular, more and more concerned with the English landscape, with the pikes, otters, hawks and crows of England, with merry England gone.
>
> Is it any wonder that a very English and very insular poet like Betjeman is Poet Laureate, and that all English poetry after the war seems to take its bearings from Betjeman's disciple, Philip Larkin, and from Ted Hughes, who in violent desperation attempts to impose his myths on us and to wrest an identity for England? Indeed it has been argued that Larkin and Hughes make up what one might call a composite British poet, if such a creature were possible. One is soft, Norman French, concerned, nostalgic; the other is tough, Anglo-Saxon, assertive, imposing. One represents British gentility, the other British 'masculinity', virtues appropriate to the Imperial character. What Larkin in his neutral and modest way seems to be saying is that it is a pity the soldiers could not be maintained and had to be brought home from their duties abroad. What Hughes seems to be saying is that this is no time for self-pity or nostalgia. This is the time to assert ourselves as we did in the good old days of empire. Hughes's violent imagery is closely aligned with that other side of British society — the side which says 'keep England British'. Together these poets are saying in their different ways the same thing.[5]

As Lucas goes on to point out, this has particular bearing upon those Hughes poems which assert the ruthless predatoriness of nature — a conception of nature apparently unqualified by any awareness of the human dimension. You have seen what my own view of poems such as 'Pike' and 'Hawk Roosting' is; now you might like to consider how far you would accept the argument that 'there is surely something very suspect about this use of birds and fish to explore issues as complex as the history and use of power and violence.'[6] Does Hughes's poetry in fact explore such issues? If so, how?

A further consideration arises here, which is, the precise nature of Hughes's modernism. You will recall what I said about how I see Hughes's relation with 'tradition', a relation which, despite his typically modernist impatience with history, evidently has great significance in helping to locate him as an English poet. But what does it really mean to call him that? I would like finally to direct you towards another way of interpreting Hughes's attempt to 'impose his myths on us and to wrest an identity for England' — a more positive version of what Seamus Heaney has called 'a new sense of the shires, a new valuing of the native English experience', which has come about as a result of the loss of Britain's former glories, its diminished influence in the world.

Heaney's imaginative exploration of the poetry of Hughes, Larkin and Geoffrey Hill takes as its basis the belief that all three treat England as a region' 'or rather treat their region as England — in different and complementary ways ... they are afflicted with a sense of history that was once the peculiar affliction of the poets of other nations who were not themselves natives of England but who spoke the English language.' Heaney proposes an 'England of the Mind' for Hughes, which defends a threatened identity by means of language. When his language is examined, we find that:

> Hughes relies on the northern deposits, the pagan Anglo-Saxon and Norse elements, and he draws energy also from a related constellation of primitive myths and world views. The life of his language is a persistence of the stark outline and vitality of Anglo-Saxon that became the Middle English alliterative tradition and then went underground to sustain the folk poetry, the ballads, and the ebullience of Shakespeare and the Elizabethans ... Hughes's is a primeval landscape where stones cry out and horizons endure, where the elements inhabit the mind with a religious force, where the pebble dreams 'it is the foetus of God', 'where the staring angles go through', 'where all the stars bow down', where, with appropriately pre-Socratic force, water lies 'at the bottom of all things/utterly worn out, utterly clear'. It is England as King Lear's heath which now becomes a Yorkshire moor where sheep and foxes and hawks persuade 'unaccomodated man' that he is a poor bare forked thing, kinned not in a chain but on a plane of being with the animals themselves. There monoliths and lintels. The air is menaced by God's voice in the wind, by demonic protean crow-shapes; cut off by catastrophe from consolation and philosophy ... Hughes's sensibility is pagan in the original sense: he is a haunter of the *pagus*, a heath-dweller, a heathen; he moves by instinct in the thickets beyond the *urbs*; he is neither urban nor urbane. His poetry is as redolent of the liar as it is of the library ... and what he has inherited through Shakespeare and John Webster and Hopkins and Lawrence is something of that primary life of stress which is the quick of the English poetic matter.[7]

This admits Hughes's basic appeal: to our yearning for a wild freedom which, in our highly complex, industrialized, mass society we feel we have lost, and that we might find in nature, and nature's currents within ourselves. If this is an illusion, it is a charged, ambivalent illusion; one we may need to live by.

Notes

Chapter One: Introduction (Pages 1–4)

1 'Ted Hughes', *Poetry Book Society Bulletin*, No. 15, September 1957, no page nos.

Chapter Two: 'A most surprising first book'. (Pages 4–15)

1 Ted Hughes, *Poetry in the Making*, London, Faber, 1967, pp. 19–20.
2 *Ibid.*, p. 19.
3 Ted Hughes, Introduction, *Vasko Popa: Selected Poems* Harmondsworth, Penguin Modern European Poets, 1969, p. 14.
4 Edwin Muir, 'Kinds of Poetry', *New Statesman*, vol. 54, 28 September 1957, p. 392.
5 See Blake Morrison, *The Movement*, Oxford, Oxford University Press, 1980, pp. 81–4.
6 A. Alvarez, ed., *The New Poetry*, Harmondsworth, Penguin, 1965 edn., p. 28.
7 Egbert Faas, 'Ted Hughes and *Crow*' (interview), *London Magazine*, new series, vol. 10, January 1971, pp. 10–11.

Chapter Three: 'Roots': the Poet and the Personal (Pages 16–27)

1 Ted Hughes, 'Note', *A Choice of Shakespeare's Verse*, London, Faber, 1971, p. 184.
2 Arthur Marwick, *British Society Since 1945*, Harmondsworth, Penguin, 1982, p. 184.
3 See, e.g., *Times literary Supplement*, 6 July 1967, [anonymous] p. 601; and Graham Martin, 'Poets of a Savage Age', *The Listener*, 6 July 1967, p. 22.
4 Keith Sagar, *The Art of Ted Hughes*, Second edition, Cambridge, Cambridge University Press, 1978, p. 62.
5 According to 'Ted Hughes', *Poetry Book Society Bulletin*, No. 15, September 1957, no page nos.
6 'Four Young Poets', *Mademoiselle*, January 1959, p. 35.

7   *Sylvia Plath, Letters Home*, ed. A. S. Plath London, Faber, 1975, p. 233.
8   Hughes, *Poetry in the Making*, p. 15.
9   *Ibid.*, p. 16.
10 R. Graves, *The White Godess*, London, Faber, 1961, pp. 9–14, 448.
11 Ted Hughes, 'The Rock', *The Listener*, 19 September 1963, p. 423.
12 *Ibid.*, p. 421.

Chapter Four: The Memory of War (Pages 28–43)

1   A. Bold, *Thom Gunn & Ted Hughes*, Edinburgh, Oliver & Boyd, 1976, p. 109.
2   Ted Hughes, Introduction, *Vasko Popa: Selected Poetry*, Harmondsworth, Penguin, 1969, pp. 9–10; *Poetry Book Society Bulletin*, no. 15, September 1957, no page nos.
3   Paul Fussell, in *The Great War and Modern Memory*, Oxford, Oxford University Press, 1977.
4   John Keegan, *The Face of Battle*, Harmondsworth, Penguin, 1978, pp. 288–9.
5   A point made first, and very effectively, by A. E. Dyson in 'Ted Hughes', *Critical Quarterly*, vol. 1, autumn 1959, p. 225.
6   The most persuasive example of this view may be found in C. J. Rawson's careful and well-argued article, 'Ted Hughes: a reappraisal', *Essays in Criticism*, vol. 15, January 1965, pp. 77–94 (see especially pp. 82–4 and 92–4).
7   Faas, 'Ted Hughes and Crow' *op. cit.*, p. 8.
8   Michael Hamburger, *The Truth of Poetry*, Harmondsworth, Penguin, 1972, p.310.

Chapter Five: Hughes and Tradition (Pages 43–58)

1   Hughes, *Poetry in the Making*, pp. 32–3
2   'Context', *London Magazine*, new series, vol. 1, February 1962, p. 45.
3   D. H. Lawrence, 'Poetry of the Present', 1918, reprinted in *The Complete Poems of D. H. Lawrence*, collected and edited by V. de Sola Pinto and W. Roberts, London: Heinemann, 1967, vol. 1, p. 183.
4   By Terry Gifford and Neil Roberts in *Ted Hughes: A Critical Study* London, Faber, 1981, pp. 62–3.
5   See C. J. Rawson, 'The Flight of the Black Bird', *Times Literary Supplement*, 19 March 1976, pp. 324–6.
6   Introduction, *Vasko Popa: Selected Poems* Harmondsworth, Penguin 1969, p. 9.
7   T. S. Eliot, 'Tradition and the Individual Talent', 1919, reprinted in *Selected Prose of T. S. Eliot*, ed. Frank Kermode, London, Faber, 1975, p. 38.

Selected Prose of T. S. Eliot, ed. Frank Kermode, London: Faber, 1975, p. 38.

Chapter Six: The Satire of Survival (Pages 59—75)

1   Ted Hughes, 'The Poetry of Keith Douglas', *The Listener*, 21 June 1962, p. 1069.
2   Hughes's explanatory note in *Selected Poems* p. 238 refers in error to 1970; for full details, see A. C. H. Smith, *Orghast at Persepolis* London, Eyre methuen, 1972.
3   According to Alan Bold, *Gunn & Hughes*, p. 116. New 'Crow' poems were added to the 1971 and 1972 editions.
4   Significantly, 'Notes for a Little Play' was reprinted in a 'Friends of the Earth' publication, *The Environmental Handbook*, 1971: part of the contemporary cultural context of Hughes's work.
5   'Leonard Baskin' (from an introduction to an exhibition in London in 1962), reprinted in Ekbert Faas, *Ted Hughes: The Unaccomodated Universe*, Santa Barbara, The Black Sparrow Press, p. 167.
6   E. Faas 'Ted Hughes and Crow' (interview), *op. cit.*, p. 20.
7   E. Faas, *op. cit.*, p. 16; record sleeve note by Hughes, *Crow*, Claddach Records, 1973, on which you can also hear the Crow poems read by Hughes.
8   Referred to by Holbrook, 'From "Vitalism" to a Dead Crow: Ted Hughes's Failure of Confidence', in *Lost Bearings in English Poetry*, London, Vision Press, 1977, which may be said to sum up the opposition to *Crow*, although there are many who would adopt a less extreme position.
9   See K. Sagar, *op. cit.*, pp. 113—114; J. Ramsey, '*Crow*, or the trickster transformed', in K. sager (ed.), *The Achievement of Ted Hughes*, Manchester, Manchester University Press, 1983, pp. 171—185; and Ted Hughes, 'A Reply to My Critics', *Books and Issues*, nos. 3—4, 1980, pp. 4—5.
10 Cited in M. Hodgart, *Satire*, London; Weidenfeld and Nicolson, 1969, p. 14.
11 Sagar,*op. cit.*, p. 35.
12 Hughes, *Popa*, pp. 9—10.
13 Perhaps the least unconvincing and most easily comprehensible and sympathetic account is to be found in Terry Gifford and Neil Roberts, *Ted Hughes: A Critical Study*, London, Faber, 1981, chapter 6. See also chapter 7 on *Cave Birds*, which these authors believe Hughes's 'finest book to date'.

Chapter 7: Back to Mother Nature (Pages 75—89)

1   Martin Dodsworth, 'Ted Hughes and Geoffrey Hill', *The New Pelican Guide to English Literature*, ed. Boris Ford, vol. 8, *The Present*, Harmondsworth, 1983, p. 286.

2 Edward Bond, Author's Preface, *Lear*, London, Methuen, 1972, p.v.
3 'Ted Hughes' (interview), *Guardian*, 23 March 1965, E. Faas, 'Ted Hughes and Crow', *op. cit.*, p. 9.
4 G. S. Fraser, *The Modern Writer and His World*, Harmondsworth, 1970, p. 79.
5 E. Faas, 'Ted Huges and *Crow*', *op. cit.*, pp. 14–15.
6 Ted Hughes, *Poetry in the Making*, pp. 123–4; Note, *A Choice of Shakespeare's Verse*, pp. 186–7, 194–7; E. Faas, *op. cit.*, p. 7.
7 For a succinct overview of current feminist approaches, see Toril Moi, *Sexual/Textual Politics*, London, Methuen, 1985.
8 Ted Hughes, 'A Reply to My Critics', *Books and Issues*, nos. 3–4, 1981, p. 4.
9 Brian Worthington, 'The best living poet?', *New Universities Quarterly*, Spring 1980, p. 204.
10 See Craig Robinson, 'The Good Shepherd: *Moortown Elegies*' in *The Achievement of Ted Hughes*, ed. K. Sagar, 1983, *passim*.
11 'Poet's Battle Against Pollution', *Observer Magazine*, 9 December 1984, p. 29.
12 Peter Redgrove, 'Windings and Conchings', *Times Literary Supplement*, 11 November 1983, p. 1238.
13 See, (for example) Leonard M. Scigaj, 'Oriental Mythology in *Wodwo*', in *The Achievement of Ted Hughes*, ed. K. Sagar, Manchester, Manchester University Press, 1983, pp. 126–153; and the same author's 'The Ophiolatry of Ted Hughes', *Twentieth Century Literature*, vol. 31, no. 4, Winter 1985, pp. 380–398.

Chapter Eight: Conclusion (Pages 89–95)

1 Hughes, *Poetry in the Making*, p. 20.
2 For the poet's own view of the central importance of writing for children, see his richly revealing talk on 'Myth in Education', reprinted in *Children's Literature in Education*, no. 1, March 1970, pp. 55–70.
3 See Catherine Belsey, *Critical Practice*, London, Methuen, 1980, especially chapter 3, 'Addressing the Subject', for a brief account.
4 'The demon-farmer's carnival', *Times Literary Supplement*, 4 January 1980, p. 6.
5 M. G. Ramanan, 'Macaulay's Children', *London Magazine*, February, 1985, cited in J. Lucas, *Modern English Poetry: From Hardy to Hughes*, London, Batsford, 1986, pp. 193–4.
6 Ibid., p. 195.
7 Seamus Heaney, 'Englands of the Mind', 1976, in *Preoccupations: Selected Prose 1968–1978*, London, Faber, 1980, *passim*. Heaney focuses particularly ont he poem 'Pibroch' in this essay.

Suggestions for further reading

Hughes is a remarkably productive poet and so if you are at all interested in his poetry you should look out for new poems by him in such periodicals as the *Times Literary Supplement*, the *London Literary Review* and *The Listener*. Since becoming Poet Laureate, Hughes has also published 'occasional' verse in newspapers, including *The Times* and *The Observer*. But the most obvious, relevant further reading to do is to go to his numerous currently available collections, most of which I have referred to already. New collections, or reprints of earlier books, are also appearing with increasing frequency — for example, the children's book *Moon-Bells* (first published in 1978), which I have not so far mentioned, has been reprinted (1987) with a new set of illustrations, and you will certainly find much that is familiar therein, such as the delightfully macabre 'Horrible Song', which concludes:

> The Crow is a hardy creature
> Fire-proof in every feature.
> Beware, beware of the Crow!
> When Mankind's blasted to kingdom came
> The Crow will dance and hop and drum
> And into an old thigh-bone he'll blow
> Ho Ho Ho
> Singing the Song of the Crow.

We have certainly met this before, if not quite in the same form. Read more of Hughes's work (including so-called children's verse, criticism and other genres), enjoy it more and understand it better; and find out for yourself what meanings it holds for you, and where you stand in relation to it.

To help you come to a further and more informed understanding of the poems in their current cultural context, you should also look at poetry by other poets (earlier and contemporary), before going on to consider criticism and comment. Apart from the suggestions made in chapter 5, you might particularly consider some of Philip Larkin's poetry, since it is often illuminatingly contrasted with Hughes's work — as was done, you will recall, by A. Alvarez in his introduction to *The New Poetry* (Harmondsworth, Penguin, 1962). In *The Ironic Harvest: English Poetry in the twentieth century* (London, Edward Arnold, 1974), Geoffrey Thurley challengly relates Hughes to the 'native English tradition' of Lawrence and Hopkins, and also to lesser poets such as Edmund Blunden and James Stephens, so this could provide a useful alternative starting-point for comparison. Alan Bold's short study of *Thom Gunn and Ted Hughes* (Edinburgh, Oliver and Boyd, 1976) offers another stimulating comparative perspective. On a more advanced level, Gunn and Hughes are compared in a chapter of Stan Smith's admirable analysis of modern poetry, *Inviolable Voice: History and 20th Century Poetry* (Dublin, Gill and Macmillan, 1982), which stresses throughout the immediately political dimension to contemporary verse, without denying the individual quality of each poet and his or her 'voice'.

For more basic introductory guidance, which focuses on Hughes himself, Keith Sagar's *The Art of Ted Hughes* (Cambridge, Cambridge University Press, second edition, 1978) is essential, despite its uncritical acceptance of almost everything the poet does or says. More careful and balanced, yet equally illuminating, is Terry Gifford and Neil Roberts, *Ted Hughes: A Critical Study* (London, Faber and Faber, 1981), which analyses numerous single poems at length, including a remarkably helpful and sympathetic account of several of the *Crow* poems. They believe *Cave Birds* to be Hughes's 'finest book to date', and argue persuasively in support of that view. Both of these books have the virtue of drawing extensively upon Hughes's own utterances; both have extensive bibliographies, to which you should go if you wish to track down more of what Hughes has written about his own or others' work. But you will find many of the basic texts in Ekbert Faas's *Ted Hughes The Unaccommodated Universe* (Santa Barbara, Black Sparrow Press, 1980), a selection of Hughes's critical writings with two interviews conducted by Faas, including that to which I have referred several times, 'Ted Hughes and Crow', from the *London Magazine* (new series vol. 10, January 1971, pp. 5–20). Especially useful are the extracts from Hughes's introductions to the poetry of Keith Douglas, Emily Dickinson, Dylan Thomas and János Pilinszky; but you should also look at the whole of his introduction to *Vasko Popa: Selected Poems* (Harmondsworth, Penguin, 1969) and Hughes's 'Note' to *A Choice of Shakespeares's Verse* (London, Faber and Faber, 1971, pp. 181–200). Hughes on record includes: *Listening and Writing* (BBC Records, RESR19M), introductions by Hughes, including readings of 'The Thought-Fox', 'Pike', 'View of a Pig' and D. H. Lawrence's 'Bare Almond Trees'; *The Poet Speaks*, (No. 5 Argo PLP 1085) on which Hughes reads nine poems from *Wodwo*; and *Crow*, Claddagh CCT 9–10, on which he reads all but three of the poems from the first English edition of *Crow*. For another good if condensed introductory account of the poet's work to date, I would recommend Calvin Bedient's succinct chapter on Hughes in *Nine Contemporary Poets* (Oxford, Oxford University Press 1984, pp. 107–151).

Stimulating and helpful books and articles other than those referred to in the *Guide* include: M. L. Rosenthal's appreciative essay on Hughes in *The New Poets* (Oxford, Oxford University Press, 1967), Stuart Hirschberg, *Myth in the Poetry of Ted Hughes* (Portmarnock, County Dublin, Wolfhound Press, 1981) and Robert Stuart, 'Ted Hughes' in *British Poetry Since 1970*, eds. Peter Jones and Michael Schmidt (Manchester, Carcanet Press, 1980, pp. 75–84). Specifically on *Crow*, you might also look at David Lodge's 'Crow and the Cartoons', *Critical Quarterly*, (vol. 13, Spring 1971, pp. 37–42 and 68); Ian Hamilton, 'A Mouthful of Blood', *Times Literary Supplement*, (8 January 1971), reprinted in his *A Poetry Chronicle* (London, Faber and Faber, 1973); Claire Hahn, 'Crow and the Biblical Creation Narratives', *Critical Quarterly*, (vol. 19, Spring 1977, pp. 43–52); and Graham Bradshaw, 'Ted Hughes's "Crow" as Trickster-Hero', *The Fool and the Trickster*, ed. Paul V. Williams (Cambridge, Cambridge University Press, 1979, pp. 83–108).

You should be aware that all the critics referred to above, with the exception of Stan Smith, take it as axiomatic that the poet's work exists as the expression of his personality. Without attempting to undermine this general approach as a possible and indeed legitimate way of reading and responding to Hughes's work, I have in the *Guide* tried to suggest some of the problems which such an approach raises.

Despite many, sometimes brilliant, attempts to advance new critical approaches to the study of poetry, the best starting-point remains Catherine Belsey's *Critical Practice* (London, Methuen, 1980).

Index